Food Down the Ages
An archaeological tour of food & recipes

Jill Eyers

Strawberries from an original acrylic

Published by J. Eyers, 2017

Printed and bound by CPI Group (UK) Ltd, Croydon, CR0 4YY

ISBN 978-1-904898-17-7

Cover Illustrations
Front cover:
Vase showing food being served in the Greek tradition
Loaf: the burnt Roman loaf found still in the oven at Pompeii AD 79
Neolithic living and cooking area: Skara Brae in Orkney. Paul Cadle

Back cover image: loaves baked for the 'Dine like a Roman' event St Katharine's at Parmoor, Buckinghamshire by Jo Pearce

Contents

Page number

The author   4

Table 1: Summary of dates and eras   5

Preface   7

Survival or gastronomic delight?   8

1.   What was on the menu?   11
Archaeology – the remains of memorable meals through the ages

2.   Cookery   17

3.   The Palaeolithic diet – facts, fads and fancies   19

4.   Hunter-gathering – Ice Age style   23

5.   The first farmers – Neolithic dining   31

6.   The Bronze Age cowboys   37

7.   The Iron Age kitchen in a roundhouse   41

8.   Roman cuisine – a taste sensation   49

9.   Anglo-Saxon – food on a plate   67

10.   Norman peasants to Medieval banquets   73

11.   Tudor treats – plus pies, potatoes and hops   85

12.   The Stuarts – suet puds, seafood and sweets   97

13.   Fancy dining Georgian style   105

14.   Victorian recipes – designed to delight   115

15.   Edwardian eating – upstairs and downstairs   133

16.   War time recipes from WWII   141

17.   Horses for courses?   147

Further reading, bibliography   151

Classical writers   152

Some important food dates   155

Places to visit   156

Roman food items   158

Anglo-Saxon & Norman words in recipes   158

Acknowledgements   158

The author

Dr Jill Eyers is Director of Chiltern Archaeology and author of many books including tour guides such as *Geology and Archaeology of Lycia, Turkey* and *Journey through the Chiltern Hills.* As an archaeologist who is both a seasoned traveller and a renowned 'foody', this was a book that just had to be written. All dishes were researched, prepared, tasted and enjoyed!

www.chilternarchaeology.com

Dedications

For my granddaughter Tamzin who is becoming an excellent baker; and my son Joe who rarely cooks, but when he does it is pure magic; and for my daughter Lisa whose imagination can create an evening meal to match the teams playing each football World Cup game, which is both intriguing and inspiring!

Other books by the author

Eyers, J and Watkins, H. 2013. *More than six-feet-under. The big dig at St Dunstan's churchyard*, Monks Risborough. ISBN: 978-1-904898-15-3.

Eyers, J. and Watkins, H. 2014. *A journey through the Chiltern Hills*. Amberley Books.
ISBN: 978-1-4456-3624-5 (print) and 978-1-4456-3652-8 (e-book).

Eyers, J. 2011. *Romans in the Hambleden Valley: Yewden Roman Villa*. Chiltern Archaeology Monograph 1.
ISBN: 978-1-904898-12-2.

Eyers, J. 2012. *Geology of the Norfolk Coast: Hunstanton to Happisburgh*. e-book only.
ISBN 978-1-904898-14-6.

Eyers, J. 2016. *The Little Tree Book*. A guide to identification of common native trees with lots of illustrations and a key. E-book only. ISBN 978-1-904898-16-0.

The *Rocks Afoot series* is available from Chiltern Archaeology or Amazon covering geological and archaeological walks.

Table 1 Dates and influences for the cuisine styles used in the book

(For dates of some notable food developments, up to modern foods, see the appendix at the end of the book)

Era	Dates and notes
Hunter gatherer 'old stone age'	People are thought to have been living in Britain during warmer periods (interglacials) of the Ice Age from **900,000** years ago. The last ice receded 10,000 years ago which is the start of the Mesolithic era and people had semi-permanent winter and summer camps. Fishing became popular with special tools from 10,000 years ago.
Neolithic ('new stone age')	**6500–4500** years ago. The first farmers planted crops along with limited husbandry, but hunting and gathering continued alongside. These people were allergic to milk, hence dairy was not part of our early diet.
Bronze Age	**4500–2800** years ago. Crop failure occurred at the end of this period due to prolonged poor weather conditions; widespread starvation resulted in a change in field layouts to accommodate more cattle rearing as a response.
Iron Age	**800 years ago–43 AD**. Culinary changes occurred due to new crop introductions and generally increased trade. Cheese making becomes important as many survivors from the earlier population were not allergic to milk. There were social problems caused by local conflicts, cattle stealing and battles.
Roman	**43–410 AD**. A major time for the introduction of a vast array of new fruit, vegetables, herbs, meat and spices, alongside new ways to cook them and new ways to dine.
Anglo-Saxon	**410–1066 AD**. Austerity to oysters. Our first villages are formed. Manors start the feudal system which organised food production alongside a rapid division in the classes with very different food available to the rich and to the poor.
Norman to Medieval	**1066–1500**. Different diets for different classes. Norman nobility enforce serfdom within their estates & an ever widening quality of diet between the wealthy & the workers.
Tudor	**1500–1603**. Raging inflation ensures rapidly rising prices; new foods are introduced by explorers and shipping merchants from far-away places and creates an exciting range of new luxury ingredients and exotic flavours.
Stuart	**1603–1714** (for England). Back to austerity with a new idea – the boiled suet pudding, eaten with another new idea – the fork.

Georgian	**1714–1837**. A flurry of etiquette manuals saw the introduction of good dining manners which sometimes bordered on the absurd! However, this era saw the birth of a great British tradition – the afternoon tea.
Victorian	**1837–1901**. Elegant recipes designed to delight and an opportunity for the 'Lady of the house' to show off her skills. Mrs Beeton led the field for recipe books showing how to do it – from what equipment to use to the final dish.
Edwardian	**1901–1910**. The era of upstairs-downstairs. Fiddly cooking for the upper classes, but some basic classics for those 'downstairs'.
WWII	**1939–1945**. Dig for Britain austerity menus and tips. People can be very inventive in making special, tasty dishes from common ingredients.

EDIBLE, adj. Good to eat, and wholesome to digest, as a worm to a toad, a toad to a snake, a snake to a pig, a pig to a man, and a man to a worm. Ambrose Bierce, The Devil's Dictionary.

Edible? Not the same for everyone. This simple Iron Age dish of oatcakes, curd cheese, hazelnuts and milk could create potential life-threatening problems for those with allergies to nuts, dairy or gluten. But for those who did not have the allergies, they were essential nutrition which ensured survival.

Preface

"Cookery is not chemistry. It is an art. It requires instinct and taste rather than exact measurements"
Marcel Boulestin

Food rightly deserves a celebration – it is more than just a nutritional requirement for survival. Every nation promotes its own cuisine with huge pride and with almost a competitive throwing down of the gauntlet to dare other nations to produce any better. The celebration can involve everything from the start of growing the crop or rearing the animal, to the end dish served at the table. The very beginning of the food process may be seen in the pleasure taken in growing, producing or selecting your food items in anticipation of what will be prepared with them. It continues with the skill of preparing and combining the elements and the sparking of the senses as aromas fill the air. But better still, it is the sheer delight of the taste experience, exploring wonderful flavours, textures and colours. This experience could be as simple as a piece of hot crusty bread straight from the oven or it could be an intricate dish prepared over hours with many blended flavours.

Food also rightly deserves a celebration revealing the changes through the ages. Changes might be due to a multitude of factors and include new discoveries, technological development, the migration of people bringing new methods of food preparation and cooking, plus the introduction of different food and crops along with new trade sources. Fashions and superstitions also play their part in what our ancestors chose to eat in the past. Fashions and fads also play a part in our diet today.

This book focuses on the changes in food grown, cooked and consumed in the UK, but it will be of interest and relevant to many countries of the world. We take so much for granted in this country and there has been a resurgence of traditional British fare, but what do we mean by 'British fare'? The content of the book may sometimes surprise you – much of our traditional food is not quite as 'British' as you think! Hopefully you will also be tempted to try some of the recipes derived from past eras, which make an exciting theme for a dinner party or to enjoy with a special friend. Exploring flavours and ideas surrounding food from ancient times is a fun, interesting and informative process. Enjoy!

Tomatoes - not available in the UK until explorers to South America brought them back in the 16th century. Roman cookery therefore never contained tomato, unlike today's Italian food.

Survival or gastronomic delight?

"La bonne cuisine est la base du véritable bonheur = Good food is the foundation of genuine happiness."
Auguste Escoffier 1846–1935, a French chef and culinary writer

A question that has been in the author's mind for some time is 'when did food for survival turn to gastronomic delight?' I suspect the answer is gradually and by experimentation. Indeed for early humans simply finding food and feeling full may have been delight enough. However, early evidence is available for unusual items in our ancestors' diets – this includes items such as wild mustard seed stuck in 40,000 year old teeth! This seed has no nutritional value at all, and so archaeologists have assumed that the seed was added as flavouring. Other plant finds include species we know today as herbal medicine and some are hallucinogenic. These rare finds indicate our early ancestors had a good knowledge of the plants available. It also indicates taking drugs is not a new experience for humans.

A second question that needs thinking about is 'when did we start to use fire and cook food?' The oldest evidence of hominids using fire (with rudimentary hearths) is with Oldowan groups in Africa more than 1.8 million years ago (Gowlett & Wrangham 2013). Evidence for the UK is not found until around 400,000 years ago, when hearths used by hominid groups were found in Beeches Pit, Suffolk. We do not know anything about the people, but at the same time another site at Swanscombe, Sussex revealed bones of Neanderthals. Over 100,000 re-worked and finely crafted flint tools and large quantities of animal bones indicate that animals were killed and butchered on site. The fen-like habitat, with nearby river channels and woodland, provided a wealth of plants, fish and animals, and it was in use for many generations. So our initial 'glimpse' at our ancestors indicates a mixed diet.

The Palaeolithic tool kit remained very simple and did not change for hundreds of thousands of years being mostly confined to large hand axes and scrapers. This large hand axe was a tool for many jobs and it was found in West Wycombe, Bucks.

With fire, food could be cooked, not just eaten raw. Cooking had the advantage of killing any parasites, it made food softer to bite and chew, but it also made it more digestible. Importantly for modern palates it also makes food, especially meat, very flavoursome. The discovery of cooking by fire was nothing short of a food revolution.

Quote: *"Acorns were good until bread was found"* **Francis Bacon.**

Raw acorns are very bitter, but chopped and roasted they can be eaten like almonds or pounded for making a paste added to thicken stews or to form flat bread.

Discovery of safe food items as people moved across different landscapes and through different seasons would be a shared knowledge for any group. Culinary embellishments such as herbs and spices would be learned by experimentation, exactly like the best chefs today. There is a distinction to be made here between subsistence food and cooking with recipes, which makes it plausible that 'cooking' started very early on with our distant ancestors. The important distinction is between 'food' which is to provide the bulk of the calories needed to sustain life, along with essential minerals, and 'recipes and processing' using special techniques combined to alter texture or flavour including the addition of herbs and spices.

1.
What was on the menu?

Archaeology – the remains of memorable meals through the ages

Archaeology is the study of past human societies and their environment. Evidence is gained by collecting the finds that our ancestors have left behind – left sometimes intentionally, and sometimes not. The evidence must be collected in a scientific way, so that conclusions can be justified. The exciting part of the job for an archaeologist is to discover something about the behaviour of people of the past. This could be how they lived, what they made or traded, what they wore or how they died. Food is an essential part of life – it therefore commands a high profile in archaeology. Studies range from the foods eaten or drunk to how they were grown, harvested, prepared, eaten or cooked. This book will show in simple ways not only the 'what' of our ancestor's diets, but also the 'what with'. It will also investigate the changes in culture and other factors that have influenced human diet over many millennia. However, the important underlying theme of this book is 'how do we know'? The content has been selected through a variety of sources – from written recipes to archaeological finds to new scientific laboratory methods of investigating the past. It is evidence based and here is a brief account of the lines of evidence used to substantiate the knowledge of what our ancestors loved to eat, or sometimes had to eat as there was little choice.

Recipes, shopping lists and graffiti

Recipes can range from formal books to hand scribbled personal notes. Ancient books used as sources for recipes are mentioned throughout the text. These show an amazing change in style – that is not only the style of writing but the style of cooking, presentation and choices of food. Early recipes from Roman to Medieval times list ingredients, but never quantities. That is why these recipes were tested using a touch of guesswork for quantities alongside cooking skill and common sense. Texts in this category include the famous Tezelin (William the Conqueror's personal chef) and Apicius the well-known Roman foody. Shopping lists occur throughout many museum collections and the well documented tablets found at the Vindolanda Roman fort are described in Chapter 8. Graffiti is known on storage vessels – sometimes indicating the contents of the jar, sometimes a person's name scratched on the vessel (the owner?) or a shipping note.

A Romano-British girl scratched her name on the base of this greyware jar c. 200 AD. It might have been a cheap kitchen storage jar, but it was clearly special to her. Her name was Siitomina and she lived in the Hambleden Valley, Bucks.

This object may be seen in the Buckinghamshire County Museum, Aylesbury.

Coins

Occasionally coins can show an indication of foods that are either important in the diet or special by being exotic. Sometimes they have ritual significance or they may represent an emblem. In the figure below the variety of wheat can be identified.

A gold coin of Cunobelin of the Trinovantes tribe of the very latest Iron Age. The ear of wheat, which can be identified as a variety called emmer, is shown here. It's presence on a coin shows this item was of great importance to them. CAM = Camulodunum (the name of the town and location of the mint, today's Colchester). CUNO = Cunobelin, the leader of the tribe.
Photo: courtesy of the PAS on-line database: https://finds.org.uk/database/artefacts/record/id/807941

Paintings, murals and mosaics

This can be a very useful source of information although sometimes contrived as in idyllic set up rather than everyday reality. However, they can be very useful by highlighting one single aspect of a much larger scenario. Paintings of dinner tables, picnics or assemblages of beautiful food are abundant in any art museum in the country. Murals on walls of Roman houses have often given away which room is the dining room. For instance, in Roman villas Bacchus is often featured in this room along with his bunch of grapes and association with images of wine and merriment. The same is true of mosaics. However, some of the earliest depictions of food come from cave art.

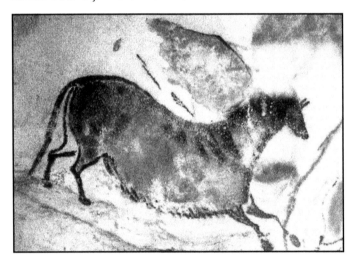

A horse being hunted a famous wall painting in the caves of Lascaux in France. The horse may be pregnant (given the size of the belly) but it is definitely a set of arrows or spears that are shooting towards it.

What's on the menu? It seems like salmon was at L'abris Pataud in France. Food items are common themes in Palaeolithic rock art.

Cooking pots and utensils

Styles of food processing give a strong indication of what might be done with the ingredients. For instance grain and grinding stones together informs us that flour was made with that grain, although it might not tell us what was made with the flour. The appearance of fire hearths informs us when we first started cooking rather than eating everything in a raw form. Cut marks on bone tell us how an animal was butchered and hence what might be cooked with it. Similarly, when a tool is used for a purpose – whether it is a stone tool or a metal knife, there will be wear or tiny marks remaining on the implement. This has led to a whole area of specialised research called use-wear analysis. The tiny abrasions and style of wear would, for instance, be able to tell whether a stone axe were used for chopping wood, or whether it was used for cutting bone, meat or vegetables.

Pots are especially valuable information for all sorts of reasons such as dating, technology, trading routes, cultural and other interesting facts. However, in relation to food – it is clear that the pots were designed for a certain job and this also reveals the type of dish cooked, the method of cooking or the other products made (such as cheese).

A cheese press (with holes to drain the whey) with a variety of other drinking and storage vessels from the Roman period (archaeological display in the Ashmolean Museum, Oxford)

A Roman whiteware flagon. Pottery items are useful to interpret their purpose, but in addition they can be dated accurately. Where their manufacture area is well known, this can indicate who is trading and with who. This item was made at Verulamium (St Albans today) and traded over a wide distance. Item: from the Buckinghamshire County Museum Trust collections

Sometimes items are not to be found at the original site and objects can be found in odd places such as this Roman sandstone quern found making up part of a much younger wall in Bucks. However, querns are more valuable when found on the original site as they provide information on trading and grain used.

Residues on pots

Pots have sooty residues on the outside when used as a cooking pot – the soot builds up as it nestles in the hot ashes or embers for a slow cook. Pots that were used for heating water tend to have a calcareous residue on the inside, especially in hard water areas. Cooking or storage pots can have food residues left adhering to the insides. This is why archaeologists always look for residues before washing the pottery collection discovered during excavations. If they did not then this valuable evidence will be washed down the sink! Even if there is not a visible residue, if the pot has been used for the same purpose over a period of time, then food chemicals can penetrate the vessel – fats are particularly good for this. However, occasionally contents of pots can be preserved if burnt or they have been covered in waterlogged conditions where there is no oxygen.

Food remaining in a Roman pot provides absolute evidence of diet and also how some foods were stored

Middens and scattered grain

If conditions for preservation are favourable then grain can be found remaining in driers, grain stores, on threshing floors, in storage vessels or maybe just scattered on a surface by accident.

A Roman grain drier which was used for malting barley. We know that malting barley was at least one of the uses, as some grain was burnt and remained preserved in the structure for 2000 years. This also provides further information that they made ale on the site. Photo: © Buckinghamshire County Museum Trust, Yewden villa 1912.

Waterlogged deposits

A special site for archaeologists is where the ground has been permanently waterlogged. This means rare organic finds including food items and wooden implements may be preserved. This provides rare glimpses into a more complete assemblage of finds.

Organic items preserved in waterlogged deposits in Cambridgeshire: from top left: wood, spruce cone, bracket fungus, acorns, cherry stones, a hazelnut, hawthorn and briar thorn (from a display at the Ashmolean Museum, Oxford).

Environmental analysis

Ancient soils, as well as infill of pits and ditches on archaeological sites, are now very commonly sampled for the organic remains that they may contain. Pollen, seeds, woody fibres, tiny bones and other items may be retrieved from bulk samples that are either dry or wet sieved. The different fractions reveal certain aspects of the site. This can be as varied as finding pips or tiny fish bones from a meal to pollen from surrounding crops and the local environment. The pollen is not only precise evidence of crop species, but indicates if the site is surrounded by pasture, scrub or woodland for instance.

Human bodies

The human body is a potpourri of archaeological information. In individuals such as the 'Bog Bodies' where preservation is exceptionally good, then the stomach contents themselves reveal direct evidence of diet – or at least the last meal of the individual. However, the bones and teeth alone can reveal longer term evidence of diet along with sex, age, height, health, diseases and accidents. This also allows an investigation of how diet may have varied between higher and lower status people, but also between male and female, children and adults. Traditions and customs may become clear by these studies – as food is not always a logical choice of 'what was around to eat'. Isotopes measured in teeth may give an indication of changes in the source of food in the diet. For instance carbon (and to a lesser extent nitrogen) isotopes give an indication of how much protein in the diet comes from seafood or land animals. Changes in these isotopes in teeth can also spot agricultural changes such as changes from animal to plant diets, and it can even spot plant changes (in say wheat and corn).

Strontium and oxygen isotopes in tooth enamel also reflect geography and they record the area where people grew up or migrated to until their early twenties. It can therefore be used to detect locals from migrants. Teeth are useful again in another way, as before toothbrushes calculus was able to build up on teeth. It is from small seeds and food fragments incorporated into tooth calculus that we have some valuable evidence for Palaeolithic diets.

Cesspits and coprolites

Of course, what goes in the body comes out and on a regular basis. As well as informing us of the social organisation and hygiene of such features such as cesspits and latrines, it also is a very useful source of information about human infestations and diet. The dietary information comes from undigested parts of meals, for instance fruit pips turn up a lot.

2.

Cookery

What is cookery? Why cook? It is more than just making food safe for consumption. It is more than tenderising tough cuts of meat or flavouring bland seed or grain. Maybe the French have it right according to Ruskin above – it can be art. It requires knowledge of different fruit, vegetables, meat and fish – and what to do with them. It necessitates a thorough knowledge of herbs, spices and combining them all successfully.

Perhaps nothing can be as stimulating to the senses as the smells and colours of the spice market.

Cookery is about being inventive, plus skill in execution! Cookery can be spontaneous, with quantities chosen by the cook using experience, but the less experienced require recipes. We have all gone into the kitchen with a wild air of improvisation, combining a 'bit of this' with 'a bit of that'. Sometimes the result is pure delight; sometimes a tragic mistake. We have also all flicked our way through a recipe book or two. Recipes conjure up anticipation and dreams. They can help us deliver those dreams by revealing some of the rules, and hopefully the dream may then be repeated on another occasion – if you write down and keep the recipe!

Cookery books start with the Romans (e.g. Apicius), but we were cooking very well before Roman recipes were written down. What did we eat and how do we know? This is what archaeologists find out for a living, and what follows in this book is an insight into this knowledge and some delightful recipes (plus some authentic recipes that are not so delightful – but there are warnings attached to these!).

"Tis an ill cook that cannot lick his own fingers." **William Shakespeare, Romeo and Juliet.**

3.

The 'Palaeo diet' – facts, fads and fancies

 This modern diet fad is meant to copy for us the diet that our distant ancestors would have eaten during the Palaeolithic period. This is also called the 'Stone Age' diet or 'hunter-gather' diet where much of the food is gathered from the wild and eaten raw.

"Tell me what you eat, and I will tell you who you are." **Jean Anthelme Brillat-Savarin**

The Palaeolithic diets that abound in our media today are really anything but 'palaeo'. A few examples of the real diet are used as examples below, but this is not for the faint-hearted! Then read on with Section 4 for the actual evidence of what our Palaeolithic ancestors ate. To be fair, there are some good pointers to healthy eating for us within our distant ancestors' diet, but the 'Palaeolithic' covers a massive period of time – from our evolution millions of years ago to just 10,000 years ago. A lot changed in the diet over this time. Without doubt the changes made us healthier, and ensured our taste for good flavours developed into our present diet. In contrast, some of our present diet leaves a lot to be desired – as our natural preference for the higher calorie foods (developed during millions of years of evolution) has out-matched our exercise. During the entire Palaeolithic period we were hunter-gatherers.

The changing point to settling down and farming came from 6,500 years ago – the Neolithic period. However, the massive change of diet, with the adoption of some very bad habits, came during Tudor times. This is the point that our obsession with sugar started. We gave up our hunter-gatherer lifestyle generations beforehand, along with the calories that the search for food expended. Unfortunately our early evolution has favoured a desire and liking of certain foods which are energy foods (high fat, high sugar). These foods are fine in small quantities when they are hard to find, but today they are too readily available. These high calorie foods were once rare finds, but they now replace many of the healthier items our evolution geared us up to eat.

The bulk of our diet used to be lots of plant fibre and carbohydrate as provided by roots, vegetables, fruit, nuts and grain. Green vegetables would have been a major part of the diet and up to 3 kilograms per day is estimated to have been the amount eaten each day, but only providing up to around 700 calories. However, this is only healthy where this food was supplemented by carbohydrates or meat which provides a healthy body-building amount of calories, protein and essential minerals. Strangely, the 'palaeo-diets' available through those posing as health gurus today, often recommend the complete abstinence of foods that used to be essential for our Palaeolithic ancestors – carbohydrate as found in roots and grain and small amounts of meat.

Scientific evidence for diet is now emerging from a number of research sources. Analysis of dental calculus has shown that a large variety of plants including grains and grass seed, tubers and mushrooms (probably *Boletus*) were eaten – as the remains of these foods have been found encrusted on the teeth of Late Palaeolithic people (dated to between 15,000 and 10,000 years ago; Power *et al.* 2015).

Despite there being a real problem with some people's modern diet, the real palaeo-diet would most certainly not be to our modern tastes (given our usual conceptions of what is tasty and acceptable to eat). In addition, the plants available today have changed enormously over time. The vast majority of food was seasonal, which left people wanting of calories at certain times of year. Extreme hunger was regular, if not constant. This period of our evolution was a long time before we settled down and farmed – everything was gathered, hunted or scavenged. The 'palaeo diet' you find in books or on websites today is often a misguided, imaginary concept using modern ingredients, false ideas, and designed only to earn money for those writing and promoting it!

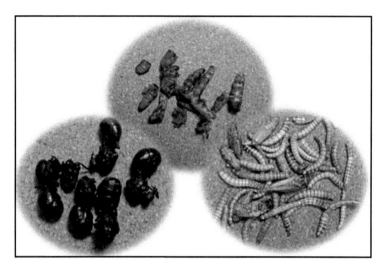

Insects and their larvae are easy to harvest and highly nutritious. Today this food source is being promoted for the future as insects have the potential to feed an ever growing human population. Insects are highly nutritious sources of protein and essential minerals. We know ancient people added insects to their diet as fragments of them are found embedded in tooth calculus, e.g. scales from a butterfly wing and insect legs (Hardy et al. *2016).*

Modern palaeo-diets often promote a vegetarian or even vegan lifestyle. However, books often depict our hunter-gatherer ancestors tucking into large carcasses of meat. Along with many other misconceptions is the fact that meat formed a large part of the diet. Animal bones are easier to find on some archaeological sites than plant or fish evidence, and this has biased the scientific record somewhat. However, it is not disputed that meat was a highly important contribution to the diet when available. It was very important to gain access to high calorie fatty meat, full of essential minerals, when the opportunity presented itself. That opportunity may well have been scavenging a dead carcass rather than killing live prey (which could also be fast and dangerous).

Chives – a tasty but seasonal herb. Full of flavour, but like many herbs and green vegetables, with very few calories. Photo: Hayley Watkins.

Archaeological evidence now uses isotopes from our ancestors' bones to detect their diet (indicating the proportions of meat, fish and vegetables). These studies can sometimes come up with surprises. Kendrick's Cave in North Wales, UK (Richards, 2005) showed people 12,000 years ago acquired 30% of their protein intake from marine mammals. In other studies meat was low down the menu, probably through abundance of seasonal other sources (plants or fish). However, some sites such as Gough's Hole in Somerset UK show a high intake of meat. Clearly where hunting opportunities presented themselves in abundance, then our ancestors took advantage – isotopes analysed in bone collagen proved that Bos species were popular (probably the extremely large and ferocious auroch, an ancestor to our modern cow) and Servus elaphus (red deer).

A final note to those wishing to keep to a strict 'palaeo-diet' – before the use of fire, all meat (including the offal) would be eaten raw. The meat from ancient breeds had a lot more fat than modern breeds, the latter providing very lean meat in comparison. However, game meat has more omega-3 and less saturated fat, so health-wise it is a case of swings and roundabouts.

There are other dietary issues. The 21st century palaeo-diets often propose we should avoid gluten. Why? Unless you are a coeliac there is no reason to avoid gluten, and no supporting evidence whatsoever. In fact the archaeological evidence shows strongly the opposite view – we were processing grain and eating it from at least 30,000 years ago in several European sites (Revedin et al. 2010; Mahoney 2007). The evidence is seen in fibres trapped in teeth and by microwear studies of teeth which have been damaged by grit – the grit derived by grinding grain with stone tools. Bones and teeth are essential for these studies and skeletons of this age are rare, but nonetheless more evidence is building up of a very varied diet. The evidence shows that we were food processing very early in our evolution, the advantage being that this releases calories by making food digestible. Calories equal survival. Further hard evidence for our Palaeolithic ancestors processing grain are finds of a variety of grinding stones with actual grains and starch remaining on them.

In addition, Palaeo-diets often propose avoiding dairy foods. This is based on our ancestors not being able to digest lactose. True – but only up until the end of the Neolithic. Our first farming ancestors were lactose intolerant. However, the gene mutated and led to the survival of groups of people that led to a large proportion of us. They survived due to the very fact that their diet was improved by eating dairy food, which provided a wealth of vitamins and minerals along with very valuable protein. The lactose intolerant gene still exists in our population and, of course, those people should not eat dairy. For the rest of us it is very definitely beneficial in reasonable quantities.

Finally, the modern Palaeo-diet menus include foods that were not available to our Palaeolithic ancestors – so how can these items have formed part of our natural 'palaeo-diet'? Some of the foods suggested in modern texts were only available in some remote parts of the world at that time – so as an example, how useful is an Indonesian diet to the widely different European Palaeolithic descendants today? It all depends whose 'palaeo' ancestors we are hoping to copy for the diverse populations of today maybe?

APPLE: n. A fruit, for eating which the first man was justly turned out of Paradise. For, the first apple being a crab apple, the first man was an idiot for eating it.

Ambrose Bierce, The Devil's Dictionary.

Palaeolithic menu – select from the list as seasonally available!*

- **Sea kale roots, seaweed and limpets (if you live on the coast)**
- **Nettle soup (flavoured with alliums such as wild leek, wild garlic or chives)**
- **Birds eggs (wrapped in moss to steam on fire embers)***
- **Boletus and Chanterelle mushrooms**
- **Beetle larvae, grasshoppers, butterflies and other insects**
- **Frogs, crayfish as available, land snails**
- **Meat would be a much rarer opportunity – but scavenge some left over wolf kill if found (today's road kill?). If your diet is earliest Palaeolithic then this would be raw.**
- **Green salad: Leaves as seasonally available: cresses including watercress, ground elder, Shepherds purse, garlic mustard, chickweeds and mallows**
- **Wild cabbage (sea cabbage), sea beet and wild asparagus**
- **Blackberries, crab apples**

*It is strongly recommended not to include wild birds eggs which is illegal, other wild animals are either illegal or require licenses to kill, and some plants are easy to mistake for other poisonous forms. Some popular wild food books are recommended for guidance at the end of this book. Road kill must be freshly obtained and not previously nibbled by other animals. It is recommended to choose modern alternatives which can be purchased in a safe and legal form if you want to give the Palaeolithic a try!

Sea kale. This is a cabbage-like plant that grows in sandy areas by the sea. It is very bitter, even if only the new young shoots and underground portions are selected. Our ancestors could eat this raw, or it may have been boiled. Today we would want to toss it in butter or coat it with a hollandaise sauce perhaps, but the flavour would still remain rather too bitter for most peoples' tastes.
Photo: Hayley Watkins.

One massive false assumption in many modern Palaeo-diets is that our ancestors did not make alcohol. I am sorry to inform these misguided 'advisors', but as soon as we had containers to do it – we brewed alcoholic beverages (and animal skins will suffice for this purpose!). We also seem to have learned about narcotics even before that time too.

Conclusion? In no way, and in no form, would I recommend the real Palaeo-diet to anyone, unless they wish to die young!

4.

Hunter-gathering – Ice Age style

This is the real palaeo-diet – anything in season that did not poison you, but the survivors learnt to avoid it when it did!

"Every investigation which is guided by principles of Nature fixes its ultimate aim entirely on gratifying the stomach" **Atheneaus, 2nd century Greek 'foodie' writer.**

What did we eat until we settled down as farmers 6,500 years ago? For the last four million years the human family have hunted and gathered their food from wild sources. Food would have been gathered to process later and for sharing with the rest of the group, but a lot of food would have been foraged and eaten whilst on the move – we evolved browsing. This means that berries, seeds, roots, nuts, fruit and fungi would seasonally form a large part of the diet. It is difficult to source a precise 'menu' for this chapter partly due to rarity of the evidence, but a short list was added to the end of Chapter 3. Also many of the plants and animals are extinct, evolved into different varieties, or no longer exist in the wild in Britain. Hopefully some of the suggestions gathered safely and legally, will provide a flavour of the time.

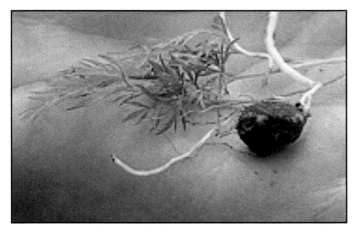

Pignut – a common hunter-gather snack. This perennial plant remained a common snack from prehistory through to Victorian times. The nut has to be dug up, as pulling the plant simply breaks it off. The root swelling or 'nut' is brown and the size of a walnut with a white inside. It can be cleaned and eaten raw or cooked by simmering. The flavour is said to be similar to celery and hazelnuts. However, it is illegal to dig up these plants now without special permission.

How do we know what ancient people ate when no written records survive? Sometimes archaeologists find a campsite or a burial and tools, grinding stones and other rare artefacts have also been found that provide a glimpse into diet. Teeth and bones are an excellent way of studying the long-term diet and nutrition of people. One way is to look at the wear patterns on the teeth – the presence of vertical striations on the sides of teeth indicate a high intake of meat in the diet, whereas horizontal striations are more pronounced in a more vegetarian diet. A second way is to look at isotopes in the teeth. The isotopes of carbon as well as nitrogen can be used to detect the amount of seafood versus meat in diets. Carbon can also tell us a lot more such as shifts in a plant diet e.g. a shift from wheat to corn would be detectable. Strontium isotopes give environmental information relevant to diet as well. Malnutrition or illness can be seen by x-raying bones. Much of this kind of research has informed this and the previous chapter.

Scots Pine *– our only truly indigenous pine. The pine cones hold small nuts which can be extracted by nail-breaking work for a tasty, nutritious but tiny snack.*

Grain played an important part of our diet from very early times. It could be collected for grinding and to use later, for instance to make a kind of flatbread. There is evidence for grinding flour to make simple bread of this type dating from 30,000 years ago. At the coast shellfish would be available, as well as seaweed and roots of salt-tolerant coastal plants, along with seabird eggs and meat on rare occasions, as and when it became available. Some of the latter might be scavenged rather than hunted. The choice of food would depend strongly on seasonal availability and selection would be learned in order to avoid poisonous items. Taste would have come into the selection process at a very early stage in human evolution as many poisonous foods also have a strong bitter flavour, and bitterness is a taste not to most peoples' liking. However, not all food was selected for nutritional purposes – items such as wild garlic and mustard seed have been found as archaeological food items. Mustard seed has little nutritional value, but has a strong and attractive flavour. Culinary skills were clearly learned early on as seeds such as these and other flavourings have been found in Neanderthal and contemporary Cro-Magnon teeth (more than 40,000 years ago).

Cooking with fire seems to have come about in Africa by 1.8 million years ago (Gowlett & Wrangham 2013) and in the UK by 400,000 years ago. A good method of doing this is to dig a pit, placing stones within the flames or embers to get hot. The meat or roots can then be placed on the stones (this works well as long as they are fatty or the food sticks to the stones). Food could also be wrapped in thick leaves on the hot stones. This method, as well as burying wrapped food in the hot embers, is still used by nomadic tribes today. It is only when our ancestors started making hearths that we can recognise their use of fire; when it was more rudimentary the evidence simply would not be preserved or recognised as being made by hominids. Hence the use of fire may well have occurred earlier than 1.8 million years ago.

Hunter-gathering requires a territory large enough to support the group. Groups were thought to vary from small families of around 10 people to larger clans of up to fifty. Some areas abroad seem to have supported larger hunter-gatherer groups, but this size group would need to be in a productive area with food available in abundance throughout the seasons. As an example, for an average temperate climate, it is thought that 8 square kilometres would support a family of 10 people; 10 square kilometres for 50 people and 30 square kilometres for 100 people. The size of the land does not expand in even increments per head as it is thought that larger groups develop more economical and successful ways of foraging than smaller ones. However, the actual size is very variable and depends on a combination of terrain, seasonal variation in weather and overall climate. The essence of successful hunter-gathering is to get the maximum return in terms of calories and nutrients for the minimum expenditure of energy.

That is the theory – what of the evidence? Evidence is difficult to come by for our early ancestors. In the UK the earliest tools to survive are c. 900,000 years old. These are flint tools and come from an ancient forest floor now part of the Norfolk coast. This was during a warm interglacial period that we call the Cromerian. Stone tools survive in the archaeological record, but unfortunately food, skin, bones and wooden vessels, which might be used for collecting or preparing food, do not preserve. Indeed, at this early stage of our history these people were not modern *Homo sapiens* providing us with evidence of occupation or hunting – it was their (our) distant ancestor *Homo heidelbergensis*.

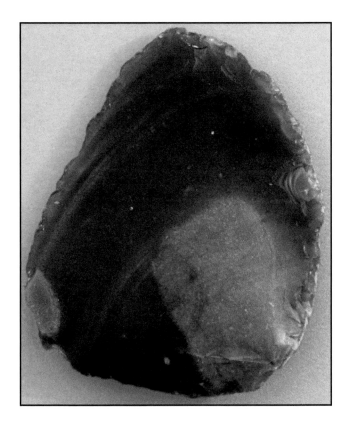 

Crude tools of c. 900,000 years old found in an ancient forest floor deposit in sediments preserved in Norfolk. 1 is a scraper or could be used as a knife 5 cm long; 2 is a multifunction tool and could be used for digging, prising, piercing or many things, like the Palaeolithic Swiss army knife!

The earliest evidence for food preparation is from the famous site at Boxgrove in Sussex, which at that time was next to a lake. This site provides a rare glimpse of some of the animal species living with our ancestors 500, 000 years ago such as familiar deer, horses, owls, hare, frogs, geese and hedgehog, but surprisingly also bison, lions, hyena, elephants, rhinoceros, wolves and cave bear. Many of the bones from excavations at Boxgrove showed butchery cut marks. The numerous tools found on the site showed the animals had been skinned, dismembered and de-fleshed at the point of kill. However, new discoveries from ancient bones around the world indicate that our ancestors may have scavenged from lion or other animal kills. Some of the larger bones had been smashed to allow marrow to be removed before discarding. Marrow is renowned as a speciality from many cultures today – try the Italian dish Osso Bucco to discover how good it can be as part of a meal.

Marrow bone – highly prized food and highly nutritious. Marrow was never wasted and smashed bones indicate the method of extracting it.

Although the archaeological record reveals evidence of animals that have been butchered, it is unlikely that meat formed a major part of the Palaeolithic diet for every group. Gough's Cave (Somerset) is an exception and was mentioned in Chapter 3. Plants would have been the mainstay. No evidence is available for how these were processed, but a wide range of seeds, berries, roots, nuts and leaves would have been available seasonally. From this list it is the roots that, for the UK, would have been a very important food source. Roots are packed full of carbohydrate and hence a good energy source. They can also be harvested and dried for carrying or storage.

Roots require much energy to dig up, whilst seeds offer an easy to gather food source. However, despite being easy to gather seeds have the disadvantage of being hard to digest. Many plants are poisonous and some mostly poisonous, but with an edible part. Death must have accompanied some of the discoveries of what was, and what was not edible! For instance, the wood and marsh horsetails (Equisetum sylvaticum and E. palustre) are easily identified plants. The green parts and rhizomes are poisonous, but there is a bud at the tip of the rhizome that can be harvested in October (for the wood horsetail) and November (for the marsh horsetail). When boiled they have a texture of potato with a slight hazelnut flavour.

Seeds are a good and usually safe source of calories. However, unless seeds are ground up to make a flat-bread or porridge they tend to pass through the gut undigested. This fact has been very useful to archaeologists, as gut contents preserved in 'bog bodies' or within coprolites have revealed some of the ancient diet of those people.

Fat-hen is a very common plant that would be harvested for future use, rather than an on-the-spot snack.. The fatty seeds could be used to make gruel and the spinach-like leaves eaten raw or cooked. The leaves have a tangy broccoli flavour. The seeds formed part of the last, probably ritualistic, meal fed to Tollund Man (whose perfectly preserved body, including the whole stomach contents, was found in a Danish Bog in 1950). Fat hen was a good choice of food for our ancestors, being rich in iron and protein, and widely distributed all over the country – as it still is today.

Our early Palaeolithic ancestors all lived through the Ice Age (2.6 million to 10,000 years ago). During this time there were many warm periods and these were broken by intense cold as ice sheets advanced towards or covered the UK. As each cold period developed (known as glacials) previously rich forests gradually changed to grassland and finally developed into tundra. Due to the cold and change of vegetation the people, along with the animals and plants they depended on, migrated southwards into Europe. When climate warmed again (the interglacials) hunter-gatherer groups naturally followed animals and plants as they re-colonised, returning to the UK. For this reason each glacial period has no evidence for human populations at all.

Palaeolithic recipes? We have none. Try to be imaginative with a fire pit and some of the following foods:

Wild game, a range of insects, watercress, wood sorrel, angelica, pignuts (note: it is illegal to dig these up today), wild parsnip, stinging nettles, wild carrot, mint, wild garlic (Ramsons), buttercups, wild thyme and marjoram. If you are at the coast you will have access to seaweed, shellfish and samphire. For dessert try the indigenous fruit selection of wild strawberries, bilberries, blackberries, crab apples and elderberries, as in season.

Be careful to select ecologically, legally, hygienically and safely – plants can be toxic! Some of this list is available commercially (e.g. the edible insects, samphire, seaweed and watercress) and this is a safer suggested route for obtaining the ingredients rather than foraging.

Mammoth are now extinct the last small herd dying out on Wrangel Island in Antarctica only 4000 years ago (after Stonehenge and the Pyramids were built! It has been suggested by several researchers that humans may have accelerated this or even been responsible for their demise. Mammoths have a very long gestation and care period for their young. This makes populations vulnerable to predation and, when low in numbers, they will not recover from even a small amount of predation. But in human terms one kill would mean a lot of meat and resources for tools such as ivory, bone and sinew. Photo: Hayley Watkins.

The Mesolithic period starts at the end of the Ice Age until evidence of people settling down as farmers – dating from 10,000 to 6500 years ago. This period saw people beginning to settle into summer and winter camps, but this was still very much a hunter-gatherer lifestyle. However, a new innovation came about – learning how to fish with specialised tools. Until this point, fishing tools had seemingly not been employed to obtain additional food from marine or river sources. Fishing barbs and hooks record a revolutionary technique at this time, as do isotopic analysis of bone which indicate an increase in fish or other marine mammals (for those groups at the coast – possibly seals or other mammals).

The tool kit for the Mesolithic was hugely added to by innovations. This is a selection of scrapers. Notable amongst the many tools are microliths (tiny pieces of worked stone and bone) for hunting spears and fishing harpoons, a variety of scrapers, backed blades (used for making knives, arrows and other composite tools), and burins for working bone and antler. Also, notched tools appear and were probably used for stripping bark to make baskets or cutting tendons for multiple uses.

The plant food available to our ancestors would have been the fore-runners of modern species. For those that still form a part of our diet (notably some berries, fruit and herbs) the flavour is simply not the same as our ancestors would have experienced. In fact many of the flavours of the ancient plants, the same species that led to related varieties today, were far too bitter for modern palates. It is amazing to think that crab apples, with their distinctive acidic taste, were the only tree fruit available 10,000 years ago in the UK.

Living as a vegetarian hunter-gatherer in Stone Age Britain would have been impossible. There was not sufficient protein or calorie-rich plant foods seasonally available. Finding at least 3 kilograms of plant material per person per day would be a huge task – it would expend much energy and provide only around 700 calories. It is clear that meat and/or fish or other items such as eggs would have been essential for survival. Large animals are much harder to seek and kill. The small animals often incorporated into the diet were rats, mice, birds, frogs, insects and other invertebrates, which were far more frequently available than large game. As a result the temptation for recipes was resisted in this chapter!

The remains of butchered bones of deer and wild boar would indicate these to be a popular part of the diet. As bones of dogs are also numerous from this time, archaeologists believe that the bond between humans and dogs was put to good use to hunt game animals from this time onwards, and maybe even earlier. At archaeological sites where dog or horse bones have been found there is no evidence of them being eaten (no butchery marks on bones) and so it is assumed the use of these animals was for other purposes on the whole. Of those animals eaten (deer, auroch, mammoth, wild boar, etc) it was more than just the meat that was of value – every part of the animal would be put to use. From skins for clothes or shelter to bone and tendons for tools, everything was used.

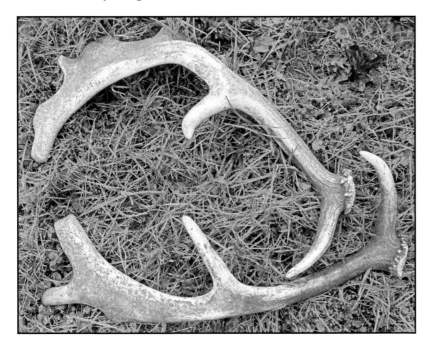

Deer antler. At a Mesolithic site, at Star Carr in Yorkshire, sets of deer antlers had been made into head-dresses. Not essential for survival, but a rare glimpse into a ceremony or ritual that was important to these ancient people. More commonly they seem to have been used as tools for instance digging, using them as a pick.

A final note for this section – it should be remembered that we hominids have been hunter-gatherers for 99.8% of our entire existence on this Earth, and surviving increasingly well on this diet. Beware – we are not used to our modern lifestyle of sedentary living and high calorie fast food – read on to find out where it all started going wrong…….

5.

The first farmers – Neolithic dining

 Hazelnuts become a favourite whilst still hunter-gathering. They were allergic to milk, but with bread, other crops and meat from farming by these early settlers did well.

From 6,500 years ago people began to settle and become farmers. Small areas of land were cleared and we discovered how to plant our seeds and keep some animals. Stable isotope analysis has startled the archaeological community by showing a very rapid, widespread change from a fish, game and hunter-gatherer diet to domesticated plants and animals as people progressed from the Mesolithic to a Neolithic lifestyle (Milner 2004). Palaeobotanical studies have shown a dramatic decrease in reliance on wild plants during the Neolithic (Colledge and Conolly, 2014). A flow of knowledge is indicated by the fact that farming ideas progressed swiftly from the eastern 'fertile triangle' of today's Iraq and Syria to the west (Europe). At first thought to be the result of communication through trading, it is becoming clearer now through DNA and isotope analysis that people themselves were very mobile and emigrated.

Although people started settling into permanent houses during the Neolithic, large numbers of animals would not have been kept in the way we run modern farms – as during the long winter months these animals would require feeding. It is likely that young animals were brought on 'for the table' during the winter months. Eating them during the winter solved two problems – food provision for the group at a lean time, whilst reducing the number of animals requiring maintenance with grazing. Isotope analyses from a site in Gloucestershire (Hedges et al. 2008) showed that 75% of the protein for this Neolithic community came from meat sources. Contrary to popular belief we did not milk animals – it has been proven by genetic studies that Neolithic people were allergic to milk. Those people today who are allergic to milk products still carry this Neolithic gene.

So what did they eat in the Neolithic? Hunter gathering from the wild larder was still practiced, and indeed has continued to the modern day, albeit in reducing importance over time. Crops could be sown, nurtured and harvested – allowing for a greater quantity than by foraging alone. However, meat was now more readily available as keeping animals removed the chance element from hunting alone. Hunting would still continue as there would be far more variety and quantity in the surrounding woods and fields. For Britain in winter it must have been a wonderful treat to have meat at the time less plant food was naturally available. This extra productivity allowed for a larger population per acre. It also allowed spare time to be used in creating finely worked tools, pottery items for storage and cooking. It even allowed time for luxuries such as art and building monuments. Monuments testify to strongly held beliefs and to meeting places – and these can still be seen today as a whole series of wood or stone henges and circles as well as significant earthen mounds and tomb burials.

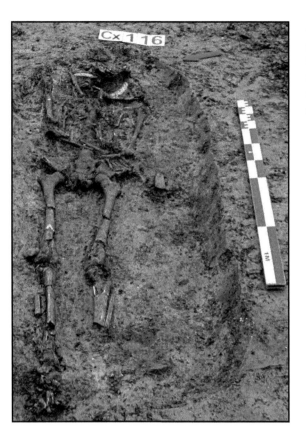

Neolithic burial (left). Bones are very useful to archaeologists in many ways, but one of those ways is to allow isotope analysis which will reveal dietary preferences for, say, ratio of seafood to meat to vegetables. In this burial there are pots buried with the body – these often contain food or residues which also provide information on diet. Photo: Doru Bogdan.

Stonehenge (below): a well known example of a monument started in the Neolithic as a wood henge and then developed further in stone. It is surrounded by a whole landscape of trackways, ditches and burials. Winter celebrations were as important as the summer solstice. Nearby, at Durrington walls, was the site of the village where feasting took place for the mid-winter solstice. The Neolithic 'Christmas' was celebrated with ritual feasting of barbequed pig, roast beef and a meat stew. The evidence is a mass of bones littering the floor areas – clearly non-one bothered to clear up after the party!

A Neolithic house at Skara Brae. The hearth can be seen in the centre of this room, with a bed to the left and the rather grand looking sideboard storage unit to the far side. The roof for this dwelling has long since decayed, but the walls and furniture are well preserved and give an insight into the communcal living of the Neolithic. Photo: Paul Cadle.

Left: part of the Neolithic tool kit – two arrowheads showing very fine and skilled manufacture techniques.

Below: A fragment of a Neolithic pot from Whiteleaf Barrow which has two imprints of Emmer grain (bottom right) included in the pottery by accident. Item: from Buckinghamshire County Museum Trust collections.

The earliest wheat crops were *Emmer* and *Einkhorn*. These grains were very difficult to separate from the ears and we very low in gluten, so porridge was the most common use for it. Bread, in the form we know it now, would not have been produced. This was due to no knowledge of yeast or other missing agent, and the low gluten grain was not suitable for bread.

However, there is evidence for a flatbread of a type similar to the Indian Chapatti or the Mexican pita bread. Barley was also sown as a crop, but oats and rye seemed to have existed only as weeds in amongst the crops at this stage. Evidence of diet comes from preserved meals in the stomachs of the famous 'bog bodies' where thickened stews had been eaten. If the wheat crops failed it is known that wild beans, beech mast or acorns could be pulverised and substituted for the wheat grains.

Charlotte age 10 cooking at a camp fire BBQ. Pieces of unleavened bread, meat or vegetables can be put onto moistened hazel skewers and rotated in the heat. A moistened stick is needed to prevent it catching fire. Cooking time is speeded up by using small cubes or thin slices of meat. Meat available was: venison, wild boar and steak (the latter would have been the massive and dangerous ancestor of our modern cattle called an auroch). Complete your hunter-gatherer meal with some baked crab apples drizzled with honey and served with wild berries in season. Or make Wild Fruit Pudding – recipe page 35.

Neolithic bread
225 g (8oz) wholemeal flour
55 g (2oz) ground hazelnuts (or pulverised beans if you have run out of your wheat harvest!)
Herbs or flavourings of choice
190-200 ml (c. 7 to 8 fl oz) warm water, enough to mix
Hazel sticks of 1 metre lengths or more, damp so they do not catch fire OR a large oiled hot rock
Camp fire

Mix ingredients in a bowl with sufficient water to make a soft dough. Knead it really well for about 5 minutes, until it is soft and elastic. Cover the bowl and leave to relax for 10 minutes or until you are ready to make the bread. Divide into small balls (small tennis ball size) and cook in one of two ways: (1) mould it around the end of the hazel stick in a lozenge shape and hold this at the right distance over the fire to cook without burning or (2) flatten balls into round disc shapes, flour both surfaces and throw it onto an oiled hot rock at the edge of the camp fire, turn until cooked through.

Hazelnuts. *Neolithic people were particularly fond of roasted hazelnuts. There is abundant evidence in the form of burnt patches where mounds of these nuts were roasted in great quantity within shallow pits. Roasting them helped to preserve them for longer periods than storing fresh nuts, although even unroasted they last perfectly well in their shell for one year. This would be a valuable food store over the lean winter months.*

Wild fruit pudding

Wild fruits (or purchased) strawberries, raspberries, blackberries, bilberries
Goat's yoghurt (<u>not</u> any other form due to Neolithic lactose intolerance)
Honey and hazelnuts

Harvest the fruits, place in a dish and liberally spoon over the yoghurt, honey and hazelnuts
Goat yoghurt is used here as it has less lactose and is more digestible than cow or sheep milk, plus making yoghurt or cheese from milk reduces the lactose, which is the allergen. Neolithic people were allergic to cow's milk and never milked them. However, they may have had goats.

Wild fruit pudding. Wild fruits are much smaller, but tastier than cultivated. You could use the American blueberry instead of bilberries, but they have much less flavour). In Yorkshire the bilberry is called the 'mucky mouth fruit' due to the staining of your tongue and lips! Photo: Hayley Watkins.

6.

The Bronze Age cowboys

Barley, beetroot and beef - as crop harvests failed cattle-raising increased.

From 4,500 years ago the field boundaries that we know today were formally put in place with ditches and banks to mark out the fields. The Neolithic people may have made some notional boundaries, but the Bronze Age people made these much more pronounced and thus the enforcement of 'ownership' of land is very clear to archaeologists. Much of this Bronze Age field layout is now marked out by hedges and fences in our modern landscape. Although there has been some enlarging and sometimes subdivision of fields since that time, the boundaries of modern farms and fields often can be shown to be, or are suspected of having, their origins in the Bronze Age 4,000 years ago.

A field system in the Chiltern Hills, the boundaries now visible as hedges and fences which were established during the post-enclosure period in the mid-1800s. Originally our field boundaries would have been simple ditches with a bank; these ditches have been maintained for thousands of years as they mark land ownership. The original Bronze Age fields tend to be roughly square in shape. Field subdivision from the larger late Bronze Age fields can still be seen on modern maps – have a look at your local area. Use of aerial photographs can show ripping out of hedges in more modern times for modern large farm machinery. By looking further back in time with older and older maps you achieve a 'map regression'. Doing this anyone can literally piece the past landscape back together over a considerable period of time.

The boundary between the end of the Neolithic and the start of the Bronze Age is almost imperceptible from evidence of diet or the style of stone tools. The era is named after the discovery of bronze manufacture and the pottery is also a different style. Both these items, when found, can date the sites. However, although used to name this era, bronze did not make its way into kitchen innovations. Kitchen utensils continued to be pottery and carved wood items or skins for cooking, storage and eating vessels. Cooking could also be by adding items (bread or strips of meat) onto preheated greased stones next to the fire (like an ancient raclette!). A popular method of cooking was to place food in a clay pot with hot wood or ashes piled up over the sealed or inverted pot. Anything could be cooked in this way from meat and grain stews to bread. Bread baked in this way is very moist as the steam is trapped. Cooking by this method is still found in Turkey and the Middle Eastern countries – often flamboyantly breaking the pot at the table to reveal the steaming and aromatic contents.

The new tool for the Bronze Age for precision hunting – a barbed and tanged arrowhead. This is a development from the triangular point seen earlier in the Neolithic. Just 3 cm long this takes great craftsmanship to make.

Bronze Age farming developed by improving arable crops and the population grew steadily – that is, until climate took a downturn at the end of this era. The weather became colder and much wetter over many successive seasons. People starved as grain rotted in the fields and crops became infected with the fungus ergot. All this information is preserved very well in archaeological botanical records. However, grass grew very well in these wet conditions and people adapted by re-shaping the original fields to be larger and hence to accommodate more cattle. They produced large herds for meat – we became the 'Bronze Age cowboys'. Today's breed known as Red Ruby is possibly the closest animal today to those bred during these times. However, cattle were not the only meat on the menu there is archaeological evidence for sheep (mutton), pig, horse and dog. Evidence from isotopes within bones indicate that fresh fish was not a major if any part of the diet, but Celtic beans, pignuts and cabbage were common vegetables. Very few herbs and spices were available compared to today's selection, but wild garlic, thyme, mustard seed and, perhaps surprisingly, coriander grew in abundance in the UK. A firm favourite over many millennia, and packed full of vitamins and minerals, is the abundant stinging nettle. Wooden bowls and spoons have been found on Bronze Age sites such as Flag Fen and may have been used to eat simple dishes such as nettle stew or beef and barley stew – both recipes are below.

Bronze Age people had made some simple ovens (a hearth type or pottery vessels under hot ashes) which could cook bread more like our loaves today. We had also learned to use barley in the first ales to be brewed (note that these drinks were 'ale' and not beer, as beer requires hops which were not used until the 16th century).

Bronze Age menus

Drink: water or ale
Nettle Stew
Beef and barley stew
Cabbage with pignuts
Assorted seasonal green leaves
Beetroot with wild garlic
Hot stone raclette (strips of steak, pork with flatbread)

Nettle stew

Combine the leaves, herbs and vegetables as available locally and seasonally:
2 bunches young nettle leaves, 1 bunch watercress, 1 bunch sorrel
1 bunch dandelion leaves, 1 bunch wild garlic or chives
2 good handfuls of barley flour
Salt (allowed for the late Bronze Age and it suits modern tastes)
Method: Chop all leaves fairly finely, mix with barley flour and salt and gradually stir in sufficient water for a good flavoursome stew quantity. Simmer for 15 to 20 minutes and serve with chunks of bread.

Beef and barley stew

1 kg (2 lb) stewing/braising beef (retain bone if you have it)
50 g (2 oz) dripping
1 kg (2 lb) Selection of veggies in season: broad beans (a substitute for Celtic beans), wild celery, peas, mushrooms, parsnips (a substitute for pignuts)
Herbs: a good handful of whichever one is in season (spring: wild garlic, summer: thyme or if coriander leaves are to be used then reserve these until the last minute).
1 litre (2 pints) water
A handful of barley
30 g (1 oz) wholemeal flour for thickening

Cut the beef into the size pieces preferred. Seal by browning in a little dripping. Add all other ingredients (except any coriander leaves) to the pot, including all meat bones.
Cook for the required time to ensure it is fully cooked and tender (an hour or more if kept simmering on a very low heat – do not boil). If uncovered top up with water as required, but allow the mixture to reduce sufficiently to concentrate the flavours.

At the end of cooking mix the flour with a little of the liquid and return to the stew, stirring all the time until thickened. Add the chopped coriander leaves (if used) and serve with thick chunks of wholemeal bread and a fresh batch of real ale.

Beef and barley stew – a hearty and tasty meal. Photo: Hayley Watkins.

Pot boilers are simply stones collected from local fields or river gravel deposits and their use is ingenious. They are put at the edge of the fire to get hot, and then hurled into the pot of stew using sticks as tongs to transfer them. The heat from the pot boilers is transferred to the stew and the dish comes to a high heat much more quickly than if simply left in ashes at the edge of the fire. The downside is that when they are very hot, and the stew is still cold, these stones can shatter – leaving the meal with numerous rock fragments in the food (a disaster waiting to happen to teeth if the stew is not eaten with care!).

Beetroot Bronze Age style

Small beetroot, as many as needed

A handful of peas per serving, direct from the pods

Bunch of finely chopped herbs & spices: wild garlic, chives, a little mint or mustard

Break the leafy tops off the beetroot (which can be reserved for stews or salads) and similarly reduce the roots by pulling off by hand (never cut these off with a knife as the colour will bleed out too much).

Wash the beets free from soil but leaving the roots intact. Cook the beetroot by simmering in enough water to cover.

Cook the shelled peas – these only need a couple of minutes to ensure they are not overcooked.
Drain and skin the beetroot. Leave whole, slice or roughly cube as preferred. Add the peas.
Sprinkle generously with the chopped herbs and serve.

7.

The Iron Age kitchen in a roundhouse

 Meat roasts, stews, cured ham and cheese, bacon, barley and beans washed down with ale; communal cooking in the roundhouse hearth.

The population grew steadily after the late Bronze Age slump. As seasonal climate improved, crops returned to successful and more reliable harvests. Beef remained a popular food and cattle stealing became a big problem during the Iron Age. Fighting between tribes was common place from at least 2,800 years ago, possibly fuelled by dwindling resources due to a large growth in the population. The diet remained very simple and rather bland to our tastes. The only reasonably abundant and flavourful herbs available were still coriander, mint, wood sorrel, tansy (very bitter) and thyme, plus spices such as mustard seed could add a bit of a 'kick' to a dish.

The Iron Age 'kitchen' – the cooking area was the hearth in the centre of the communal roundhouse. In books this is traditionally shown as a cauldron hung over the fire and also a spit set up for roasting whole animals. However, this is mostly incorrect as cauldrons are very rare finds for the Iron Age and they were probably only used for special sites, and for special people (Green, 1998).

Cooking jars are numerous finds on Iron Age sites. Slow-cooked stews can be been perfectly cooked in these vessels, nestled in the embers of the hearth. Joints of meat and cheeses were smoked by hanging them from the beams in the roof void where smoke from the fire would rise and linger before gradually filtering its way through the thatch. A perfect all-in-one cooking, preservation and storage system!

An Iron Age cooking pot clearly showing the soot from the fire. Item: from the Buckinghamshire County Museum Trust collections.

The focus for main meals was three-fold: either roasts or stews (including soups) or porridge-like dishes. Iron Age food remained mostly local produce and highly seasonal with additional preserved smoked cheeses and bacon. The smoking process was easy as the items could be hung from the rafters of the round house where the smoke from the fire would permeate continually. The Iron Age love of cheese and milk products did not go unnoticed by the Roman Empire, who looked down in scorn at this consumption.

"Most of the tribes in the interior do not grow corn but live on milk and meat, and wear skins."

Julius Caesar

Various writers in Rome made critical comments that the Northern nations (= the Celts and Barbarians) were "milk drinkers and eaters of butter". This intended insult says as much about the Romans as it does about the Celtic nations. However, it is unlikely that huge quantities of fresh milk were drunk as, with no refrigeration, the milk would soon go off. It is known that cheese was highly prized by the Iron Age people in Britain, which seems to have been almost as popular as their bacon and salt meat – both widely traded across Europe. Butter can be presumed to have been stumbled across by accident whilst transporting the milk and shaking it on the uneven tracks. A similar mishap might be envisaged for the first cheese, if milk were transported in a useful 'container' such as an animal stomach. The natural rennet within this container would soon have set the milk to curds.

Archaeological evidence also suggests that soft curds were often made by coagulating milk with nettles or sometimes rennet from sheep stomachs. Perforated bowls are common items from excavations where the curds and whey could be separated by draining. The curds were then flavoured by smoking them or adding berries, nuts, honey or herbs such as wood sorrel or mint.

Porridge-like dishes and stews dominated the diet and these were made in large cooking pots using a central open fire. On the coast the Iron Age diet could be supplemented by limpets, mussels and other shellfish, seaweed, samphire, sea kale, and scurvy grass (the latter resembles asparagus). On the whole, fish and shellfish remained only a small or no part of the diet for inland tribes. Away from the coast, there is evidence of woodland hunting for small birds, wild boar and deer. Remains of broken eggshells show that nests were plundered and birds were a popular source of food in general. The bones of many species of bird are found on archaeological sites including swan, duck, pigeon, quail, red grouse, plover, blackcock, corncrake, heron and a multitude of smaller birds including all the songbirds, red kites, kestrels, ravens and crows.

A fragment of a strainer for cheese-making. Pottery bowls with perforations such as this are believed to have been used to separate the whey from the curds. They are common finds on Iron Age and Roman sites.

A small round of rustic cheese, made in a similar way to the Iron Age method. The precise flavour of the cheese would vary enormously due to the 'lucky dip' element of what micro-organisms are naturally in the milk or present in the preparation area. Today we use a starter culture to get a particular type of cheese.

Woodland foraging provided seasonal vegetables including tasty wild asparagus, celery and carrot (a white variety as the orange colour was genetically selected much later on) and beetroot, wild parsnip radish, turnip, watercress, peas and celtic beans (tiny broad beans). Also available in the woods were elder, sloe, dewberries and other berries, fungi, wild vetch as well as herbs, and nuts such as hazelnuts continued to be an important part of the diet.

Crab apples were the only apple, but wild cherry, wild garlic, dandelions and clover all added flavours and variety to an otherwise rather bland diet. There were not any of the basic fruit trees or vegetables that we know as 'British' today, as these were not introduced until the Roman invasion in 43 AD!

Three generations of carrot – the purple and white wild varieties and the 16th century cultivated orange carrot that we mostly eat today.

The meals were washed down with mead and ale. There was no wine making and no olive oil until towards the end of the Iron Age. It was only at that time, these commodities became part of trading barters with the Roman Empire.

A carinated cup from the latest Iron Age to earliest Roman period, very early 1st century – a period that was often called 'Belgic'. Item: from the Buckinghamshire County Museum Trust collection.

By the Iron Age a more hardy type of wheat called Spelt had been discovered which would survive a winter sowing and hence provide more food with this early crop supplementing the later emmer planting. The rotary quern invention made grinding grain much easier. This was introduced about 400 BC and grain stores were a common feature in settlements by this time.

A fragment of a saddle quern with grinding stone. With time the 'saddle' shape with its characteristic central depression is worn by continued grinding of grain. This was a very lengthy process and a lot of hard work was required to gain relatively small amounts of flour. Some skeletons (notably of females) show arthritis of the shoulders, back and knees compatible with being the main grain grinder for the family. This is seen from the Neolithic to Iron Age particularly. During the later Roman and Medieval periods more energy efficient querns and mills were developed. Item: from the Buckinghamshire County Museum Trust collections.

There were two ways to store grain – either up high in a hut on stilts (to keep rats and mice from the grain) or buried in pits. These pits were large and were very effective in grain storage. They worked on the principle that once the top was sealed the outermost grain would sprout in the pit due to the moisture found in the rock or clay there. Once sprouted it would use up oxygen and give out carbon dioxide. If sealed effectively then no further air could enter and hence the bulk of the grain was preserved until the pit was re-opened.

The grain store reconstructed at Butser Iron Age village in Hampshire.

The large quantity of cattle bones found in some archaeological sites, notably southern England, is indicative that young animals were slaughtered for beef and older animals kept as milking herds. The cattle would have been a Celtic shorthorn type – the nearest breed today is probably the Dexter. A very popular meat was the domestic pig, but venison was now a rare meat in the diet, as deer kept further away from areas of habitation. The hunting of deer then began to take on more of a sport appeal than a necessity for food.

A storage pit for foods reconstructed at Butser Iron Age village. The housing (left) covers the pit (above) which at this site was dug into chalk. The temperature could be maintained much lower and steadier than ambient air temperature.

Sample menus for the Iron Age

Drink: water, mead or Celtic ale
Mussels and limpets impaled on sticks and grilled over the fire
Damper bread (using spelt wheat and ground black bindweed seed or fat hen seed)
Roast spatchcock of pigeon with samphire
Bacon and bean stew
Leaf salad (plantain, mallow, dandelion, Good King Henry)
Honey curds with roast hazelnuts and oat cakes

For a special occasion a spit roast beef joint could be added.

Roast spatchcock of pigeon with samphire

Pigeon, 1 per person, prepared
Herbs in season (thyme is best)
A little ale
Dripping
Sourdough bread
Samphire (washed to remove all grit)

To prepare the spatchcock yourself, cut down either side of the back bone and remove bones and then flatten out. (Today it is easier to ask your butcher to do it!)
Place pigeons in the ale with herbs to marinade for at least one hour
Melt dripping in a pan and fry 1 minute per side, pressing the spatchcock down to brown evenly.
If the pan is not suitable for transfer to the oven then transfer the spatchcock to an oven-proof dish and put in a hot oven for 6 minutes.
Place a slice of bread per person in the pan, soaking up the juices.
Place the pigeon on top of the bread and return to the hot oven for about 3 minutes.
While the pigeon is cooking add the samphire to boiling water. Cook for only 3 to 4 mins, drain.
Serve the pigeon on the golden bread, sprinkle with further herbs and serve with the samphire.

Bacon and Bean stew

250 g (8oz) streaky bacon, chopped
500 g (1lb) broad beans (a substitute for similar smaller celtic beans)
3 celery sticks
250 g (8 oz) parsnips (a substitute for pignuts)
250 g (8 oz) mushrooms, boletus and other endemic fungi were available
500 ml (18fl oz, just over ¾ pint) water
Teaspoon of mustard seed
Handful of Thyme

Only use very young broad beans or the skins will be hard and leathery. Fry the bacon in the cooking pot, browning it and releasing some fat.
Add the chopped celery and parsnips frying long enough to soften slightly. Add the mushrooms, beans, water, thyme and mustard seed, Stir well. Cover and simmer gently for about 1 hour.

Bacon and bean stew. Photo: Hayley Watkins.

Honey curds with roast hazelnuts and Oatcakes

Oatcakes:
500 g (18 oz) medium oatmeal
250 g (9 oz) stone-ground wheat flour
60 g (2 oz) dripping or lard
1 teaspoon salt (for the late Iron Age dish)
Water

Mix the flour with the oatmeal, add salt and rub in dripping or lard. Gradually add enough water to make a dry dough. Shape in the hands and press to make flat cakes (makes 10 to 12).

Cook in a pan or griddle until a pale-golden colour (about 10 mins).
These can be served with cheese, but here the suggestion is for a dessert with curds and drizzled with honey.
A recipe for curds can be searched for (with whole milk and rennet) but today it is easier to simply purchase fromage frais. Decorate with the honey and chopped hazelnuts.

Honey curds with oatcakes. Photo: Hayley Watkins.

8.

Roman cuisine – a taste sensation

Anything you want and can afford – sumptuous and as flavoursome as you can make it – lots of salt and sauces; washed down with wine.

"Let food be thy medicine and medicine be thy food" **Hippocrates**

Roman evening meals in wealthy houses were sumptuous affairs. Even the poorer households had access to much tastier food than the much blander Iron Age diet. Courses were often composed of many smaller dishes. The meal would start with a burst of many delights (promulsis), all highly seasoned and often mixing sweet and savoury ingredients together in the dishes. Two courses might follow with several choices in each. These were commonly presented as the first main course (primae mensae) followed by the second course (secundae mensae). Desserts were a rarity and not usually offered as a separate course, but often offered as part of the secundae mensae. Fresh fruit or items such as shredded lettuce were popular as digestives at the end of the meal.

Food was eaten at low tables, seated on cushions on the floor. There were no forks in use yet – fingers were into everything - for sampling the dry food or by mopping up juices and sauces with bread. The size and style of dishes and plates indicate changes in eating habits over time. In the early years portions were served on individual plates. Over time large dishes and plates became popular for communal eating – with everyone tucking into the shared dish, with fingers and bread. A style still used in some parts of the world. For those that could afford it – the spoon came into use for the dining room, but never in the kitchen.

The Roman kitchen – kitchens became a separate room within the main building with well equipped specialised areas within it for storage and charcoal cooking. Villas in the 1st century still cooked over hearths – similar to the Iron Age tradition. Then braziers became common followed by wood fuelled ovens later on. High status villas such as the palace at Fishbourne had specially designed charcoal ovens. The kitchen was probably not very clean and would be smoke filled with lingering cooking smells.

A Roman kitchen as part of the display at the Verulamium museum (St Albans). The indoor rooms of simple villas would normally be rather dark as window would be very small or not present at all (window glass was for the rich only). Spot the mistake?

(Orange carrots were not around until after 1600. Roman carrots would be white or purple!).

Cooking implements became specialised for new methods of preparing food such as mortaria for grinding and mixing the new style sauces, and frying pans (patellae) and other pots and pans (e.g. patinae deep pans) were added to the kitchen equipment. Large jars remained popular for cooking dishes in the hot ashes of the fire – a style continuing from the Iron Age. Black Burnished ware was well known quality cooking ware of the day – a bit like Le Creuset today. This was made by the

Durotriges tribe in Dorset and traded over wide distances – even as far north as Hadrian's wall. Once cooked, a three-legged cauldron and portable pottery ovens could be used to bring dishes to the table and keep them hot. The era of fine dining had begun.

A mortarium for grinding ingredients and blending the new style flavours for adding to dishes or to use as pouring sauces. This impressive Samian mortarium would have been a prized possession for the Roman villa owners at Hambleden, Bucks. However, it is puzzling to archaeologists why Britain used far more mortaria than anywhere else in the Roman Empire (even in gastronomic Rome). It has been suggested (based on sheer numbers, wear analysis and places they are found - such as pit offerings and temples) that the mortaria were often far more important than mere kitchen equipment. They may have been taken on for special cultural roles or be part of religious rituals. Buckinghamshire County Museum Trust collections.

A large jar suitable for slow-cooking a stew or other food while nestled in hot ashes. Cooking jars are recognised by a sooty appearance on the base and sides where they were firmly embedded in the hearth ashes.

A selection of pottery for mixing, serving and cooking food which formed part of set of cremation grave goods left for the deceased. Burying items such as this has meant sets of whole contemporary items are found together and in good condition. Items are from Wendover and held with the Buckinghamshire County Museum Trust collections.

Equipment such as ladles, spatulas, sieves, skewers, cleavers and other specialist items made the kitchen much more elaborate and encouraged new styles of preparation and serving. Even knives had a make-over with carved decoration of bone, wood or horn handles.

Cleavers were a Roman import and were used to butcher meat (Iron Age people used knives for the same purpose). This type of cleaver was for chopping, not slicing. Photo: by courtesy of the PAS online database https://finds.org.uk/database/artefacts/record/id/83388.

A carved bone knife handle. The metal blade has not preserved, but the handle is still intact. Item: Buckinghamshire County Museum Trust collections.

Much of the older literature, and especially in ancient accounts such as the novel The Golden Ass by Apuleius (2nd century AD), depicted Roman eating as one of gorging at sumptuous banquets until the diners were sick and then returned to start again. Apuleius describes feasting on stuffed dormice, larks tongues, braised flamingo and a wide variety of fine dining with lashings of liquamen and garum (both sauces made from decomposing fish in brine, but an absolute Roman favourite!). Dishes were unbelievably salty or over-sweetened with honey, often mixed all together – sweet and savoury in the same dish. The record states that massive over-consumption of food was washed down with so much wine that the eaters could not

walk without the help of their servants. This may have occurred at some exceptionally rich and decadent households in Rome, but archaeological evidence of eating styles and food choices for the masses is one of a more moderate consumption, albeit with some 'odd' selections and recipes for modern tastes.

Walnuts. The Romans thought walnuts were food sent by the Gods.

In contrast to Apuleius' account there are many other surviving texts on food coming from Rome showing the link between health and food. In this respect many recipe books were written by physicians and specifically indicated the medicinal purpose of some foods. Unfortunately most of these texts have not survived, but an important manuscript comes from Galen (AD 129 to c. AD 210), who was the personal physician to the emperor Marcus Aurelius.

He was a prolific writer and amongst his surviving works is what he believed to be the definitive guide to a healthy diet. This was based on the theory of the four humours (which are linked to climatic factors that regulate the body: hot, cold, wet and dry). Some of his recipes and medical advice are included in the recipes below. These ideas continued right through to the Medieval period and into Victorian Britain.

The only surviving written evidence for food ingredients in Britain (other than graffiti on pots acting as labels for the contents) comes from the Vindolanda tablets. The Vindolanda fort on Hadrian's wall has given a wonderful glimpse of army life at this time. The text on writing tablets of the day is now available to search on-line where many interesting insights into everyday life can be found. These range from a letter accompanying a gift of socks sent to a son from his mother, to an invitation to a birthday party, while another is a possible shopping list (below) given to a slave:

"... bruised beans, two *modii*, chickens, twenty, a hundred apples, if you can find nice ones, a hundred or two hundred eggs, if they are for sale there at a fair price. ... 8 *sextarii* of fish-sauce ... a *modius* of olives ... (Back) To ... slave (?) of Verecundus."

The translation is from the Vindolanda website Dec 2016 . Inventory no. 88.839.
[1 modius = 8.6 litres (18 pints), so this is rather a large amount to carry back from the market!]
Another tablet (TVIITablet:208) is part of a recipe which lists olives, garlic, spiced wine or pickling liquor and salt. This seems a tasty way to preserve the olives. An intriguing piece of Vindolanda graffiti is a jar indicating it contained precisely 1884 coriander seeds! Strange information to scratch onto the jar, which suggests the counting was a small punishment task maybe?

Little written accounts such as these give a valuable insight into the tasks and food of the day. However, written accounts are very rare. In contrast to the paucity of the written evidence, there is an abundance of archaeological finds providing evidence for the food eaten in Roman Britain. Information comes either directly from food items preserved by charring or buried in anoxic conditions, or from the residues in containers used for food. There are also pollen analyses from soils surrounding villas testifying to the crops grown nearby as well as natural vegetation. In addition, archaeologists regularly sieve the sediment filling Roman waste pits and ditches during excavation work. This careful work discovers everything from whole carcasses to tiny pips and fish bones.

Charred spelt grain from Yewden villa. Emmer wheat continued to be used in Roman Britain at first, but this was soon replaced by spelt wheat crops. Rye also became a common crop and was prized as fodder for sheep. Two-row barley was grown for ale making and feeding to animals, particularly horses.

Very importantly, there is also the written record such as recipe books written mostly in Rome. One famous recipe book De re coquinaria (meaning 'on cookery') dates from the 1st century AD and either was either written by Apicius or the book was dedicated to him. A glimpse of Roman recipes shows that many are not tuned to our modern tastes - being too salty, too sweet, too peppery or all three of these! Some recipes use techniques we would not undertake today, for instance Pliny recorded that Apicius recommended for really tasty pork liver destined for paté, that the pigs be fed with dried figs and killed by an overdose of honeyed wine (known as *mulsum*).

Some ingredients are also illegal to gather or kill today, and these recipes have been adapted for this book. Some of Apicius' recipes are actually quite similar to recipes that are common-place in Italy today and many are fairly simple to make, which makes them ideal to try out in today's busy lifestyle. Importantly, he gave the name 'recipe' to us for the instructions for a culinary dish, as he starts each instruction with 'Recipe...' which is the Latin for 'Take...'

Although his name is now synonymous with gastronomy, Apicius actually gave very vague instructions in his 'recipes'. There were never any quantities, and no times for cooking were given nor the best temperature. It is also clear, that when the recipes were received in Britain, some instructions such as those for cooking a flamingo (recipe below) were not going to be much use without this species being available. However, the influence for the flavours devised by Apicius (along with many other chefs and medics writing in Rome) was very pronounced in Britain. This can be seen by large quantities of new style food ingredients reaching our shores, along with new forms of pottery and kitchen equipment. This was achieved by wholesale 'selling' of the lifestyle by Rome – we willingly became Romanised. That is why, for Britain, it is more accurate to call the inhabitants during this period the 'Romano-British' as the population continued to be the locals, but living in the new Roman style. There were extremely few 'Romans' in Britain (e.g. people from Rome), the population being locals under the control of Rome enforced by the army and client king network.

Beef, mutton, pork and goat were all very popular. Pork especially was very popular and Apicius provides 17 recipes for pork. Goat was preferred while young and suckling pig was a special banquet meal. Cattle and sheep were mostly eaten as older animals, so veal and lamb were much less on the menu than today. Bos taurus (a short horned variety of Highland cattle) was a popular breed. Selective breeding in Roman times produced a type of sheep resembling the North Ronaldsay today.

Poultry such as chicken, ducks and geese were first introduced to the English diet by the Romans. Although they were reared, they remained low on the menu of many villa households. They seem to have been a high status food – appearing more in rich villas or on military sites. Apicius provides 15 recipes for chicken. Surprisingly, game such as wild boar and deer was not eaten very much except in a few very high status villas. Hare was a little more common. Horse bones are fairly common finds on archaeological sites, but it is extremely rare that they show signs of being eaten. That is, there is little evidence such as butchery marks. It appears the Romano-British did not eat horsemeat. The exception to this rule is a special temple site (Turner, 1999) at Witham in Essex, where there were lots of butchery marks indicating consumption. Reasons have been put forward ranging from a cult activity to simply a large available supply and a taste for this meat in the area.

Fish was much more expensive than meat. There was very little marine fish in the diet for urban households and presumably this was due to a lack of refrigeration. Where they are found it is nearly always herring, sea bream, flounder, plaice and grey mullet. Evidence of lots of mackerel bones seems to be linked to large amounts of fish sauce production. However, freshwater fish are found much more often – species such as eels, salmon, trout, perch, pike and roach were popular. There are sites with ponds and a freshwater input diverted to them – these are highly likely to be fishponds for breeding or at least storing fresh fish until needed.

A Roman oyster found in Buckinghamshire – a good distance from the sea to be transported safely without refrigeration.

One notable favourite for the Roman diet seems to have been oysters – oyster shells are found in great numbers at most villa sites, even if they are situated well inland. The trade from coast to inland markets was well organised and oysters from the south coast, from Essex and from the Thames Estuary were transported in wooden containers, destined to be baked for a snack or *promulsis* (recipe below). The Roman population not only thought that they were an aphrodisiac, but they also had medicinal uses. Pliny described them being used for settling upset stomachs, relieving colds and cleansing ulcerated bladders. Crushed shell mixed with vinegar was used as toothpaste and crushed shell rubbed onto skin was a beauty treatment to soften the skin and to cure sores.

Food was flavoured by a vast array of newly introduced herbs and spices (see the list below). Food was so highly spiced that it was almost addictive. Pepper was essential to Roman cookery. Apicius adds it to a huge range of dishes including sweet dishes. Pliny writes of three types of pepper: black, white and a 'long pepper'. Vinegar was a common ingredient to both sweet and savoury dishes – the modern concept of sweet and sour is not new. Pliny said that rubbing a mixture of ground coriander, cumin and vinegar to meat would make it last longer in summer.

The main stays of the Roman style of cookery were olive oil and fish sauce. Fish sauce arrived in one of four forms: *garum, liquamen* and *muria* (all liquids) and a sediment called allec was also produced (see recipe below). Exactly how they differed is now not known as all information has been lost, but it is known that the source for most of Britain came from the Iberian Peninsula packaged in amphora.

In addition to the potent fish sauce, the preparation of other immensely flavourful sauces made use of the new equipment of the mortaria. These sauces combined an array of spices, herbs and berries with olive oil. The testimony of how important this item was to the Romano-British kitchen tallies with how many fragments and even whole mortaria are found in Romano-British excavations! However, as mentioned earlier, not all mortaria were used in the kitchen – some were clearly brand new, broken deliberately and placed in the top of pits. It has been suggested that this is an 'act of closure' to appease the gods of the underworld for digging the pit into their territory (the ground). This idea is supported by an array of special items carefully placed in the top of pits, mortaria being just one. Other offerings can include unusual items such as a pony head, pine martins or infants, but the precise reason behind the deed is not known for certain.

Amphorae along with a variety of jugs and a table from Pompeii. Amphora were containers used for new high status foods such as wine, olive oil and fish sauces (garum and liquamen).

List of food introduced by the Romans:
Animals: fallow deer, pigeon, doves, hare, chickens, ducks, geese.
Vegetables: asparagus, radish, turnips, parsnips, broad beans, field peas, white carrots, celery, lettuce, endive, new varieties of cabbage, cucumbers (the latter never raw, but always cooked)
Fruit & nuts: apples, pears, plums, damsons, cherries, mulberry, bullaces, figs, grapes, walnuts, sweet chestnuts. Note that Pliny said figs were food for slaves!
Herbs: fennel, garlic, caraway, cumin, summer savory, poppy seed, lovage, borage, sage, thyme, parsley, rosemary, rue, bay, peppercorns, myrtle berries.
Other introductions were imported, but not grown here such as dates, pomegranate, peaches, olives, lentils and pine nuts.

Note there is no evidence for ginger, saffron or cinnamon in Roman Britain, although they are well known to have been used in Rome and other parts of the Empire. There is evidence for the start of bee keeping during the Roman period – as honey was the only sweetener for food, it was incredibly valuable, plus it had uses as an antibacterial agent (as advised by Pliny).

Breakfast, lunch and dinner

Little is written about breakfast and so it is not certain precisely what may have been the main items for this meal. It seems likely that bread was the main component, although a variety of wheat, millet or barley porridge may also have been eaten. Fruit was always on the Roman menu and was sure to have made an appearance at breakfast. It seems to have been traditionally eaten at sunrise, for those that wanted to take this meal.

Lunch would be fairly simple, but it is thought that many people did not eat lunch. However, it was realised by Hippocrates much earlier (in the 5th century BC) that people were different. Just like today some needed breakfast, no lunch, but ate a healthy dinner. Others preferred no breakfast, but ate lunch. In indicating that people were very different, he also pointed out that some people:

"were not suited to eating lunch as they grow drowsy, start yawning and become mentally and physically dull. Should they then eat a dinner as well then they have indigestion, wind and diarrhoea."

Writers such as Plutarch, Fronto and Cicero indicate that a simple cold lunch is preferable to a cooked lunch - and eating anything rich or fried seemed to have been totally frowned upon as disgraceful! Simple lunches would consist of a variety of breads, cheese, beans, vegetables and fruit such as figs, peaches, pears and apples. Workmen would be issued with lunch on these lines. Hot lunches, if taken, could be fried fish or stews, with hot bread and cheese. However, these hot meals were often only available in fast-food establishments. In the towns it was the norm to eat out. In fact in large towns houses simply had no kitchen at all – they always ate out. Only high status people had town houses large enough, and with sufficient slaves, to have functioning kitchens.

Fast food outlet – the Pompeii MacDonalds!
Food could be kept either hot or cold in the large storage jars beneath the counter.

Dinner was a much more elaborate affair – whatever your class in society. In Roman cities it was customary to visit the baths before dinner, and often the invitation to dine with someone would be given at the baths. Outside the towns even modest villas had specially designed dining rooms. Elaborate decoration such as mosaics and wall paintings were an important part of the dining experience in wealthy villas. The highly spiced and extreme flavours of many dishes during this period would be far too salty, sweet or extreme for modern tastes and so the recipes have been adjusted slightly, except where there is a warning! The courses to a dinner party might look something like this:

Promulsis
Literally meaning 'promises' and are light little tasters to whet the appetite. This would consist of a lot of hors d'hoeuvre dishes such as olives, lettuce, cucumber, asparagus, mushrooms, eggs (for very special occasions), baked oysters, stuffed dates, grilled endive and snails. A sweet honeyed wine would be served with this course.

Primae mensae
The first main course typically consisted of dishes such as sausages, rissoles, pork meatballs, a variety of fish in highly flavoured sauces, chicken or other bird dishes (e.g. flamingo!), stuffed dormice, stuffed suckling pig and other hearty dishes. Wine diluted with water would accompany this course. Cider was available by the end of the Roman period.

Secundae mensae
The second main course might be fritters, shellfish, cheesecakes, semolina, fruit, nuts, honeyed curds or pastries. The serious drinking accompanied this course!

Symposium
An optional extra course was sometimes added to special dinner parties where a large quantity of wine was drunk with singing or dancing entertainment, along with merriment and witty banter, perhaps with toasts to Bacchus a god synonymous with wine today.

"BACCHUS, n. A convenient deity invented by the ancients as an excuse for getting drunk". Ambrose Bierce, The Devil's Dictionary

A standard Roman loaf preserved in the oven at Pompeii. Heat from the Vesuvius eruption charred the loaf completely which preserved it within the confines of the lava stone oven.

The following recipes show some good examples of dishes that were made for breakfast, lunch and dinner respectively.

Bread has been the staple of the British diet since the Stone Age. No loaf has ever been preserved in Britain, but evidence from elsewhere in the Empire shows a popular shape was a round loaf scored into eight sections. A list found in Pompeii includes 14 types of bread for sale including a loaf made with milk, pepper and oil and also a bran loaf called Pane ciberium. Pliny liked a wholemeal loaf flavoured with coriander and poppy seeds sprinkled on top. A baker shop burnt down by Boudicca in her AD 60 revolt had dill and poppy seeds which would make a flavoursome bread variety. Globi is a type of cheese bread which is spread with honey and sprinkled with poppy seeds. Below is Cato's recipe for a special kind of bread (called Placenta) that forms a whole meal in itself. Bread was baked on a griddle or a charcoal oven.

Recipes: 1. Fish sauce and bread Roman style

Fish Sauce (*Liquamen*)

You need to make a large quantity of this for it to ferment properly. However, it is not recommended due to the potential food poisoning if not carried out correctly! An alternative is to use a combination of a strong Thai fish sauce or Burgess' Anchovy Sauce.

Any fish (whole, heads or entrails) e.g. sprats, anchovies, mackerel, herring
2 pints of salt to every peck* of fish (* a peck is a dry measure of 8 quarts or 8.8 litres)
Mix this well and leave overnight, then leave uncovered in the sun for 2 to 3 months, stirring occasionally. Strain and it will be ready for use or it can be stored.

The three types of fermented fish sauce are: *liquamen, garum, muria* and *allec. Liquamen* usually has the ratio of salt to fish as between 5:1 to 1:1. Apicius often uses *liquamen* in his recipes.
Garum is the clear liquid that can be drained off and is not as salty as *liquamen. Muria* is poorer quality as it is a transportation form of the sauce comprising garum with added fish entrails. *Allec* is the sediment left at the end of the process – full of fish bones and anything not rotted. It is not certain, but this may have been for medicinal use such as treating ulcers.

Roman Placenta

Marcus Porcius Cato was the author of 'De Agri Cultura' which was a farming manual with recipes. This bread dish would have been classed as a simple lunch, and suitable for manual workers. Bread was the staff of life, and both Hippocrates and Galen used it as a medicine for a variety of ailments – often broken up in water with honey, or water with vinegar.

The outer pastry:
1 cup strong flour (plus some for flouring the surface)
Olive oil (a little for brushing)

For the tracta:
1/2 cup flour
1/2 cup spelt flour
Olive oil, for brushing

For filling:
450 g (1lb) fresh ricotta
1/2 cup honey
6 fresh or dried bay leaves

Preheat oven to 110°C (Gas mark ½).

Make the outer dough: Place flour in a mixing bowl. Dribble in about ½ cup of water, mixing well to form a stiff dough. Knead the dough for two minutes; shape into a ball. On a flat surface, roll the ball into a thin circle, approximately 30 cm (12 inches) in diameter, dusting with flour to prevent the dough from sticking. Brush both sides with oil, leave to rest.

Make the tracta: Combine the wheat and spelt flours in a mixing bowl, add water as above to make a stiff dough and then roll it into a rectangle. Brush both sides with oil, and cut into three tracta; rest.

Make the filling: Place the ricotta in a bowl; add the honey. Beat the ricotta mixture until very smooth.

To assemble the placenta: place the outer pastry round on a baking sheet. Neatly arrange the bay leaves over the centre of the circle, so when the sides are folded up the leaves will be on the bottom. Spoon ¼ of the filling over the bay leaves and place one of the tracta on top, in turn cover this with another ¼ of the filling, and so on until used up. Fold over the outer pastry so that it completely covers the whole stack. The pastry should overlap and be secured in place by wetting and pressing together. Bake for up to two hours (when the placenta will be light brown). Slice and serve warm.

Roman bread plait
A plait of bread seasoned with pepper. The milk sweetens it slightly. This could be eaten with cheese or with honey for a sweeter alternative.

600 g (1lb 3 oz) wholemeal flour
150 ml (¼ pint) warm water
1½ teaspoon yeast (use dried for convenience or fresh if available)
1 teaspoon sugar
200 ml (7 fl oz) milk (cow or goat)
60 ml (2 fl oz) olive oil (the Romano-British would probably use lard or butter)
1 teaspoon pepper

Dissolve the sugar in the warm water and add the yeast, stirring to mix thoroughly. Cover and leave in a warm place for about 15 minutes. Put all ingredients in a large bowl and knead for about 5 minutes to make a soft, pliable dough. Cover the mixing bowl with a plate and leave to rise in a warm place for 2 hours. Knead the dough once more and divide into three balls. Roll each ball out to a long (30 cm; 12 inch) strip. Line all three lengths up and press firmly together to join at one end and then gently plait them, moistening and pressing together at the other end also. Place the plait on an oiled baking tray and cover loosely (oiled cling film or domed cover to allow the loaf to rise for an hour in a warm place. Bake for 40 minutes at 200°C (400°F, Gas 6). This is lovely served hot from the oven and ripped apart with sweet or savoury dishes to dip into such as the Garlic and herb paté below.

Recipes: 2. Promulsis dishes or lunch snacks

A selection of nuts, eggs, olives, lettuce and other salad vegetables would be served in small dishes alongside any of the following recipes.

Garlic and herb paté
Very tasty, using local produce, and eat with hot crusty bread. Roman aristocracy thought garlic offensive peasant food, but it was a common item in most diets.

4 whole bulbs of garlic
250 g (8 oz) feta cheese
3 celery sticks
Bunch of coriander leaves
Small amount of fennel leaves or seed
2 tablespoons olive oil
2 tablespoons white wine or cider vinegar (or less)
Salt and pepper to taste

Hit the bulbs of garlic to break apart and spread out the cloves on a baking tray. Put into the oven for about 20 minutes to soften and sweeten the garlic. When cool enough to handle remove the skins. In the meantime put the celery, fennel, coriander and cheese into a blender, add the peeled garlic, and mix until smooth. Add the vinegar and oil and lend again. Serve with hot crusty bread. Note the longer the garlic is baked in the oven the sweeter it gets; the more raw the garlic is, the more pungent the taste – so choose exactly how you like it.

Lettuce fritters

This is a hot, simple starter or lunchtime snack. Use lettuce that has the most taste and that is very crispy and firm. Lettuce leaves with a lot of moisture will wilt and the result will be soggy fritters (not very nice!). This is another of Athenaeus' dishes called Catillus ornatus. These were exceptionally popular snacks. (The author is not sure why as they are bland with an odd texture and colour!).

1 lettuce, washed and fine shredded
150 ml (¼ pint) red wine
30 g (1 oz) bacon fat (or vegetable fat or lard)
300 g (10 oz) flour (spelt flour would have been traditionally used)
Plenty of black pepper
Oil (for frying)

Put the lettuce with the wine and fat in a mortarium or any kitchen bowl will do. Mix and then add the flour, with the black pepper and knead to a soft dough. Flatten out by hand onto a floured surface and cut into fritter strips (Atheneaus cuts it into thin strips, but feel free to make any shape you like). Put a shallow layer of oil into a frying pan and when hot gently fry the fritters, turning and ensuring they are golden on both sides. Season generously and serve.

Baked oysters with lovage

Oysters (3 per person)
Lovage, finely chopped
Salt and pepper

It is thought that oysters were not usually eaten raw as the shells show no knife marks for prising them open. It is much more likely that they were baked – the shells opening with the heat. Oysters were hugely popular and shells are found ubiquitously on Roman sites – even inland, as they were transported with ease in barrels or tanks filled with seawater.

Bake the oysters in their shell by placing onto hot stones or charcoal. Oysters will open naturally. Do not overcook. Sprinkle with a little chopped lovage and salt with a liberal sprinkle of pepper.

Apicius' fried snails

Note: this recipe for a starter is not recommended as it is not kind to snails. The snails used for eating are the edible snail (Helix aspersa) and the escargot (Helix pomatia), other snails are not suitable. To make this dish we recommend only purchasing snails commercially reared and already prepared for cooking.
Snails, a few per person
Milk with flour
Salt, olive oil
Asafoetida (ground), liquamen, olive oil

The recipe says to soak snails alive in milk mixed with a small amount of wheat flour (to purge and fatten them). Fry in salt and olive oil. Blend the asafoetida with liquamen and olive oil. Add during the cooking, toss and serve.

Eggs in Garum
Eggs of choice, boiled and shelled
Garum for pouring

Cut eggs in halves or quarters, pour over garum, scatter herbs of choice.

Right: Eggs in Garum. Eggs were considered an important food and were so revered they sometimes were laid as grave goods.

Mushrooms with coriander and red wine
A delicious and simple starter or party dish.

500 g (1¼lb button mushrooms
3 tablespoons fresh chopped coriander
600 ml (1 pint) red wine
Salt and ground black pepper to taste (Romans liked a lot of black pepper)

Put the wine in a pan and boil until reduced to c. 450 ml (15 fl oz). Add the mushrooms with the seasoning and then simmer for 5 minutes. Allow to cool a little and sprinkle over the coriander just before serving to get the best flavour and attractiveness of this popular herb. Serve in small ramekin dishes or on a sharing plate with cocktail sticks to spear them.

Mushrooms in coriander and red wine – simple and tasty. Photo: Hayley Watkins.

Celery and leek laxative dish
Another recipe from Apicius, but not necessarily a 'laxative' by today's standards! The use of butter in this recipe is unusual as Roman recipes always used the much preferred olive oil for cooking and as an ingredient. Butter was only normally used medicinally or as a base for ointment. This is very different to the Gaulish nations (British Iron Age) who loved butter and all dairy produce.

Large head of celery (or two small), sliced
6 medium leeks, trimmed and thickly sliced
25 g (1 oz) butter
Salt and black pepper

Put the celery in a pan just covered with water and simmer for 10 to 15 minutes until al dente. Drain but keep the cooking water. At the same time put leeks into pan and cover with water and bring to the boil, cook well until mushy and water has reduced by at least one third. Drain and also keep this water with the celery water put to one side. Mix the celery with the leeks and keeping them warm put on a serving dish. Melt the butter in a pan, adding 300 ml (10 fl oz) of the vegetable water. Bring to the boil, pour over the vegetables and serve.

Recipes: 3. Primae mensae

Apicius' baked ham

There is grafitti on the wall of an inn in Pompeii saying that the innkeeper's customers would lick the saucepan in which Apicius' hams were cooked!

2 kg (3 to 4 lb gammon)
15 dried figs (large)
6 bay leaves
1 tablespoon honey
350 g (6 oz) wholemeal flour
2 tablespoon olive oil
Cocktail sticks (wooden)

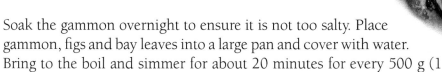

Soak the gammon overnight to ensure it is not too salty. Place gammon, figs and bay leaves into a large pan and cover with water. Bring to the boil and simmer for about 20 minutes for every 500 g (1 lb). While the gammon is cooking the pastry can be made by stirring the oil into the flour and mixing to a soft dough with the cold water.

When the gammon is cooked, lift from the pan and drain; peel off the skin. Cut this into small squares and place them with a mixture of 1 tablespoon honey which has been dissolved into 2 tbsp of the cooking liquid. Allow the meat to cool a little before rolling out the pastry to totally cover the joint, turning the pastry under at the base. Put onto a baking tray and into an oven set to 180°C (350°F; Gas 4) for about 30 minutes until the pastry is cooked. However, about 10 minutes before this is cooked remove it from the oven and stick the pieces of skin all over with the cocktail sticks. Return to the oven to continue cooking.

Prepare the figs for an accompaniment by removing them from the pan and taking 60 ml (20 fl oz) of the cooking liquid, add the honey mixture that had been soaking the skin. Boil rapidly to reduce it to about ¾ of its original volume. Serve hot with the baked gammon.

Poussin in asparagus sauce

Apicius' recipe was for a songbird called a Figpecker, but poussin is a good alternative for modern tastes and supermarkets. Apicius would have served this with a spinach salad or other vegetables.

1 kg (2 lb) asparagus
6 poussin
300 ml (½ pint) white wine
6 shallots, sliced
2 bay leaves
1 teaspoon honey
6 egg yolks
Salt and pepper

Place the asparagus into a large pan with 1.2 litres (2 pints) water. Cover and simmer for about 20 minutes until completely tender (less for young asparagus). Put some of the tips aside for decoration. Put the rest to one side whilst the water is then used for the poussin – add the birds, wine shallots and bay leaves. Simmer for 45 minutes until cooked. Take the birds from the pan and as soon as cool enough to handle remove the skin. Only the breasts are used for this dish (the remainder of the birds can be used in other dishes or soup). Place the breasts on a serving dish. Meanwhile puree the asparagus with 300 ml (½ pint) of the cooking liquid. Place in a double boiler (or dish placed in pan of water, so heat is less direct). Add eggs yolks and heat gently stirring constantly until it thickens and then add the honey, salt and pepper. Spoon the sauce over the poussin breasts and decorate with the spare asparagus tips. This method of cooking makes very moist chicken which is delicious with the asparagus. Serves 6.

Apicius' braised Flamingo

1 fresh flamingo (prepared and washed if you can catch one!) – swap for a goose?
Dill (a good handful) & a little vinegar
Leek, coriander, asafoetida root, mint, rue (ground in a mortarium)
Plump dates
Cornflour, enough to thicken the liquid to your liking
Water (ample to cover the bird)

Place the flamingo (or goose – geese were known to be reared on farms along with chicken and ducks) in a large pan, cover with water and add dill & vinegar. Simmer.
Grind the leek and other flavourings (adding a little cooking liquid) in a mortarium.
Add the cornflour to a little of the liquid and blend. Add a little more liquid. Place all in a pan and heat until thickened to a sauce consistency, stirring all the time to avoid lumps.
Serve the 'flamingo' with the sauce poured liberally over the top.

Apicius' stuffed suckling pig

This recipe is very time consuming and costly, and requires a lot of preparation. However, it must be adapted for today's more modest and legal requirements! All meat and poultry has to have bones removed.

1 suckling pig, boned
Chicken pieces, bone removed
Several small birds including thrushes (perhaps swap for quail, partridge, pigeon?) de-boned
Sausages, minced pig entrails & snails (shells removed!)
Dates, dried bulbs, mallows, beets
Leeks, celery, cabbage, pine kernels, 15 eggs (soft boiled and shelled)
Coriander, peppercorns, *garum* or *liquamen* (Thai fish sauce can be swapped for the latter).
For the sauce: olive oil, *garum*, honey, pepper and rue

Arrange all the main ingredients within the cavity of the pig and sew it together to keep all ingredients within. While the pig is roasting, combine the oil, garum, honey, pepper and rue to make a sauce for serving.

*Above: a whole suckling pig requires a large oven and support so as not to collapse.
Below: served up on a bed of bay leaves.*

Ficatum porcinum: Fried liver in coriander sauce

A recipe by Anthimus which used pigs liver where the pigs had been fattened up on figs.

500 g (1 lb) pigs liver, sliced
100 g (3 oz) flour
Fresh coriander, large bunch
Olive oil, salt and pepper

Prepare the sauce by making a purée of the coriander with 2 tablespoons of olive oil, salt and pepper (traditionally ground in the mortarium, but we can use a liquidiser today). Put some more oil in a frying pan, coat the slices of liver in seasoned flour and fry in the pan until golden on the outside by still slightly pink on the inside. Serve either drizzled with the coriander sauce or place the sauce in a little ramekin dish alongside.

Kidneys in *garum* sauce

If you like kidneys then you will enjoy this dish.

0.5 kg (1 -1¼ lb) lambs kidney (skinned and cored)
1 large or 2 medium onions, roughly chopped
30 g (1 oz) butter or glug olive oil (to fry onion & kidney)
1 clove garlic
Red wine (a big glug)
Garum (Thai fish sauce or anchovy sauce is a good replacement)
Porcini mushrooms (fresh or rehydrated dried form)
Stock (if rehydrating porcini mushrooms use some of this liquid in the stock)
Bay leaf, pepper
Parsley or other fresh herbs in season.

Kidneys in garum sauce – surprisingly tasty.
Photo: Hayley Watkins.

Fry the onion gently until soft and just beginning to colour. Add the chopped garlic and porcini mushrooms. Add the kidneys and brown gently. Add all other ingredients with enough stock to make a very shallow juice in which to simmer very gently for 20 minutes, stirring regularly and checking it does not dry and burn. With the correct quantities of liquid a thick sauce will coat the kidneys at the end of the cooking time. Remove the bay leaf. Serve with crusty bread and a sprinkling of chopped herbs such as parsley.

Stuffed Dormouse

As this is a protected species use chicken thighs instead! Use 2 chicken thighs per person in the simple recipe below. Apicius' recipe uses a pork, pine nut and *liquamen* stuffing.

Bone the chicken thighs (keep the skin on) and then stuff each thigh with one of the following:
1. Sage stuffing: breadcrumbs, onion, pepper, salt, freshly chopped sage, egg to bind or
2. An apricot wrapped in bacon
Pack tightly together in a cooking dish or tie each up to stop the contents falling out. Then roast until cooked right through.

Stuffed dormouse (chicken thighs!) – delicious.

Isicia omentata (Apicius' Roman burgers)
To make 4 large Roman Burgers or 6 smaller ones

500 g minced pork
60 g pine kernels
3 teaspoon garum (Thai fish sauce will be fine)
Handful of coriander, chopped
Handful of juniper berries (optional)
A lot of black pepper
A glug of red wine, to moisten.

Grind up the pine kernels and mix with the minced pork and all the other ingredients in a bowl.
Shape the mixture into 4 large or 6 smaller burgers.
Cook over a medium heat or barbeque for 5 minutes each side or until cooked through.
Serve plain or in a flat bread bun.

Isicia omentata here uncooked and ready for the grill or barbeque – delicious! Photo: Hayley Watkins.

Alexanders in butter
The Romans introduced alexanders to England from the Mediterranean and it quickly became naturalised and today it can be found wild in many places, especially in hedges near the coast. The young leaves (seen from the end of January) can be used in salads, but the best part is the stem. Only use the pinkish stem found lower down the plant (throw away any green stem). Cut the tender pinkish stem into pieces up to 15 cm long, blanch & simmer for 3 minutes, change the water to eliminate the strong pungent, aromatic smell. Bring back to the boil and simmer for 10 minutes. Serve with melted butter to dip into - the flavour will be just a little aromatic now.

Purée of lentils and chestnuts
A starter or a main course (for 6 or 4 respectively) – a recipe from Apicius:

225 g (8oz) cooked chestnuts (pack, tin or fresh)
Large pinch of pepper
Large pinch cumin
1 level teaspoon coriander seed
1 teaspoon fresh mint (chopped); our recipe used fennel
1 teaspoon wine vinegar
1 tablespoon olive oil
90 ml (3 fl oz) vegetable stock
Water
350 g (12 oz) red lentils
2 medium leeks (sliced thinly)
1 teaspoon crushed coriander seeds
1 tablespoon chopped fresh coriander
1 teaspoon red wine vinegar
1 teaspoon honey
150 ml (¼ pint) white wine
750 ml (1¼ pints) vegetable stock
Sesame seeds
Salt

Put the chestnuts in a pan with the pepper, cumin, coriander seeds, mint, oil, vinegar and stock. Bring to the boil and simmer for 10 minutes. Puree this mixture. Put the lentils in a large pan with the leeks, coriander leaf and seeds, mint, vinegar, honey, wine and stock. Simmer for about 20 minutes until the lentils are cooked and liquid is absorbed. Mix the chestnut puree into the lentils, season and place in a serving dish decorated with coriander leaf and sesame seeds. This dish can be served hot or at room temperature (but not directly from the fridge).

This resembled baby food as it was pureed. Mixing in some reserved half chestnuts makes the dish more attractive in look and texture.

Recipes: 4. Secundae mensae

Curds – useful for many dishes

Tasting like a cream cheese, curds were a useful way to use milk which would otherwise go off very quickly. A recipe for making fresh curds is easy to research, but today it is much easier to purchase fromage frais or Quark.

The curds may be used as a base for a variety of dishes such as adding finely chopped herbs and perhaps a little garlic for a tasty dip, or as a pudding by drizzling with runny honey.

Herb dips – made with curds with: mackerel and black pepper; pea-shoots and garum; and parsley with garlic.

Itrion - Honeyed sesame

A tasty lunchtime treat from Athenaeus
100 g (3 oz) sesame seeds
60 g (2 oz) runny honey
Olive oil for greasing a plate or tin

Put the honey in a pan and simmer for 10 minutes. Add the sesame and simmer for a further 5 minutes, stirring frequently. Spread the mixture out onto an oiled dish or plate, flattening it out with a wet spoon or spatula. Cool and allow to set for a couple of hours. Cut into slices and enjoy!

Peppered honey cake

1 teaspoon cinnamon	To garnish: chopped hazelnuts, a little honey, mead/wine
225 g (8oz) spelt wheat flour	4 tablespoons mead (or a sweet wine/sherry)
1 teaspoon baking powder*	4 tablespoons grape juice
½ teaspoon ground rosemary	1 tablespoon runny honey
110 g (4 oz) almonds, chopped	A little milk
½ teaspoon black pepper	

Mix the flour and baking powder, blend with rosemary, almonds, pepper and cinnamon.
Combine the mead/wine, grape juice and honey in a jug. Mix with the dry ingredients, adding enough milk to make a soft dropping consistency.
Bake in a 22 cm (9 inch) greased tin at 190°C (gas mark 5) for approximately 30 minutes.
Spread the cake with a little liquid honey and decorate with the nuts, prick the surface with a fork and drizzle

a few tablespoons of mead/wine into the cake.

(*A little cheat to make it more palatable for modern tastes, but natural yeasts might have been in the grape juice which may have given a little rise too.)

Peppered honey cake. This makes a heavy, but strangely nice tasting cake. When this cake became stale it was cut into slices, dipped in milk and fried in olive oil, served with yet more honey! Photo: Hayley Watkins.

Fried butternut squash
A Galen recipe which possibly used other forms of squash such as gourd.

1 large butternut squash
Plenty of olive oil
2 teaspoons oregano
Garum (this fish sauce was very popular our closest equivalent is Thai fish sauce)
Pepper
Salt (only if not using *Garum*, which is salty in itself)

Peel the squash, remove the seeds and cut into suitable pieces to your liking. Either par-boil or steam until al dente, then drain and pat dry. Put some oil in a frying pan and gently fry the squash and oregano until it is cooked and browned. Sprinkle with salt and/or *Garum* and serve.

Fruit compote
Apicius recommends any hard skinned fruit.

3 apples and 3 pears (or other fruit) peeled and sliced
½ teaspoon black pepper
1 tablespoon fresh mint
2 to 3 tablespoons honey to taste
1 tablespoon red wine vinegar
90 ml (3 fl oz) white wine
90 ml (3 fl oz) water

Put the fruit in a large pan, add pepper, mint, honey, wine, vinegar and water. Simmer for 10 to 15 minutes until just cooked (do not overcook!). Arrange on a serving dish. Can be served hot or cold (and lovely with yoghurt).

Fried bread with honey
1 wholemeal loaf
600 ml (1 pint) whole milk
Olive oil and honey (runny)

Only remove the crust if it is very hard. Cut slices into smaller portions (triangles or quarters). Soak bread in the milk and fry in the hot oil. Drizzle the honey over the bread and serve while piping hot.

9.

Anglo-Saxon food on a plate

 Two courses served on plates (often wooden): a main and a dessert, with a third starter course for the rich. Local produce (within 10 miles), but imports for the rich. Lots of woodland game, pease pottage, berries and nuts featured in both menus, washed down with mead.

There were huge social and economic changes following the exodus of the Roman army from Britain and the collapse of the monetary system as a result. Towns emptied as people went back to providing food from the land. A new wave of settlers entered the country from groups known as the Angles, Saxons, Jutes, Franks and Frisnians. Technology changed significantly as did building styles and the imports of high status foods was severely halted for some time.

The Anglo-Saxon kitchen was well stocked in the larger houses with possibly a cauldron hanging in the hearth as the main cooking area. Wealthy families could afford expensive equipment including frying pans, hanging griddles, tongs, shears, hooks and spits for roasting, bowls, plates and a variety of dishes for serving. Amazingly the plates were mostly wooden, not very hygienic. On the whole pottery was of a very poor quality as people had reverted to making pots by hand and firing in clamp kilns (effectively little better than big bonfires).

Storing foods employed a variety of flasks, buckets, barrels and bottles. Very small, poor households would not be able to risk an open fire inside their small houses, where sparks might set light to the wooden frame and thatch roofs. Small houses had oven pits in the ground outside. This took the form of a pit dug to a depth of up to 1 metre which had wood placed in the bottom. When this had been set alight, and it was burning to a red glow, the cooking could be undertaken over the pit as a roasting item or as a pot positioned above the wood and heat. Poor families might only be able to afford one cooking pot (often a 3-legged cauldron), which led to creativity and lots of pottage! A pottery dish could be used for baking items such as bread as long as it had a lid and the vessel was placed over the fire embers, and not directly into the flames. Late Saxon written records such as Ælfric's Colloquy mentioned that bread was the staple of the daily meal.

Cooking pit in the back yard of an Anglo-Saxon house in Monks Risborough, Bucks (excavated 2013 by Chiltern Archaeology). Burnt wood was removed from the blackened base and used to carbon date the pit to the Saxon period.

An Anglo-Saxon cooking pot, showing the soot left by ashes. It is crudely made and small (13 cm diameter). Pottery of this era is very poor quality and tends to disintegrate in the ground. Hence it does not get well preserved. The result is there is less evidence available from residue analysis about what was cooked in them. Item: from the Buckinghamshire County Museum Trust collections.

If the household had a cauldron then this would be likely to hold a semi-permanent soup of root vegetables, peas, beans, herbs with small pieces of meat (when it could be afforded). This could be kept on the simmer for considerable time. Poor families might only be able to add the meat bones or perhaps only vegetables, which would include lots of pulses. A pease pudding stuffed into a pig's intestine could be added to such a stock and this would be likely to have lots of herbs. Many of the Iron Age traditional methods of cooking returned such as slow-cooking in pots with lots of stews and soups became the norm again.

Pottage cooking over a wood fire – a simple dish of vegetables with bacon off-cuts.

However, the Romans had left a legacy of a multitude of new vegetables, fruits, herbs and nuts which were growing well in the fields, plus a knowledge and desire for spices. Ale and mead returned as popular alcoholic drinks, along with cider. Imports such as wine and olive oil had died away at the beginning of Anglo-Saxon times and Britain once again became the butter, milk and cheese consuming nation they had been before the Roman invasion. However, this situation did not last long. By the Domesday period in the 11th century there were 30 vineyards recorded for the south of England alone. Special goods and food supplies such as wine, oil and spices were also being imported again towards the end of the era – at least for those that could afford them.

Saxon diets would have varied enormously between the rich landowners and the land workers in the hamlets and villages. Transportation was fairly restricted on poor quality roads, but rivers would have allowed the main distribution and trading of products for those that could afford them. Nonetheless, for the most part the Anglo-Saxon villager would have had a diet which was confined to a small area (maybe a 10 mile radius or so) around their homes. Much of the food grown would be dictated by the landscape and soil. Wheat, barley and rye were staples (oats mostly used for animal fodder, although getting gradually more into household diets at this time). The standard loaf of bread was called maslin and this was a mixture of wheat and rye flour.

Other crops would include root vegetables such as turnip, carrot and onion. Pulses such as peas and beans were grown avidly and convenient as they could be stored.

Apples and pears were very popular fruit, as were nuts and a vast number of herbs. Wild food played a major part in the diet, whether nuts, berries, wild garlic and other herbs, or game such as birds, hare or wild boar. Anglo-Saxon people would be able to walk the woodland collecting seasonal food and hunting wild animals. This was about to come to a bitter end when the Normans invaded, as they took over much of the land which was shared out between William's relatives and followers. This land was subsequently made out of bounds to local people creating much resentment and anger. It led to a shortage of food for poorer people who had previously used the woods for foraging and hunting.

Broad bean Vicia faba, crimson flowering. Large field crops of peas or beans were not planted in early Anglo-Saxon times. This has been suggested as being due to such crops being very easy to steal. Crops of both peas and broad beans were at first only grown around the household. A small plot yields quite a large amount of beans which can be dried for easy storage. When peas and beans were eventually planted in fields on a larger scale, strict laws came in as to when harvesting could be done and how to do it. Harvesting of peas was called 'coddling'. Many of our place names are derived from Anglo-Saxon or Norse and so today's village names like Benacre, Banstead or Peasenhall record where these crops were being grown. Photo: Hayley Watkins.

Pigs were kept in the woods and were still a common part of the diet. Herefordshire and Buckinghamshire were famous for their pork which acquired a wonderful nutty flavour as pigs could feed on beech mast and acorns within the woodland. Sheep and cattle were also eaten, but had a valuable use for milk and for wool, and so young meat from these animals was an expensive luxury. Similarly, hens were so valued for their eggs that they were rarely eaten by anyone except the very rich (until they had finished laying when they could be used as broilers).

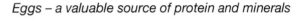

Eggs – a valuable source of protein and minerals

Fish was a considerable part of the diet. River fish were particularly important with species such as eels, trout, perch, pike and lamprey being regularly eaten. Inland there is no evidence for marine fish making up part of the regular diet. However, near the coast the favourites were salmon, cod, herring, plaice, flounder, whiting and a range of shellfish, crab and lobster. With no other way of preserving this fish (or meat) salting became a common way to treat food if it was not to be eaten immediately.

Recipes for those on modest incomes could include dishes like salt cod boiled in milk and butter, or seabirds wrapped in clay and baked in the fire. Sauces were becoming popular, especially with the upper classes. A favourite was the French-style 'green sauce' which was made with a variety of green herbs notably parsley with others as available.

SAUCE: n. The one infallible sign of civilization and enlightenment. A people with no sauces has one thousand vices; a people with one sauce has only nine hundred and ninety-nine. For every sauce invented and accepted a vice is renounced and forgiven.

Ambrose Bierce, The Devil's Dictionary.

Rich households could afford large joints of meat and a variety of different fish and shellfish. They would also have a dessert - this group of dishes was called eft mettas meaning 'after meats'. A popular dessert was a sweet pancake which was filled with flowers and/or fruit and drizzled with honey.

Ultimately, it was seasonality that was one of the major limitations in the Anglo-Saxon diet and where possible foods were regularly preserved. Fish, bacon, and beef could all be salted to last many months; grains and pulses could be dried; nuts stored; and milk preserved as cheese.

The recipes below have been informed directly from excavations where remains of kitchen equipment have been found or clues were provided by residues on pottery, as well as the form of the pot. Isotope evidence from skeletons and studies of remains from cess pits have recently contributed to current knowledge of diet. It seems that Anglo-Saxon food was indeed very wholesome and tasty!

Anglo-Saxon menu
Starter: Drewen benes (Mixed beans)
Main courses: Griddled trout with herbs
(griddled with rosemary served with crusty bread and seasonal greens)
Hare stew
Mutton pottage
Dessert: Curd cheese pastries

Griddled trout with herbs
Trout (cleaned, 1 person)
1 sprig of rosemary for each trout
1 sprig thyme & 1 sage leaf per trout
Butter
Salt and pepper to season

Place a sprig of rosemary inside each trout. Chop the sage leaves and mix with leaves from thyme (use fingers to rub off from the woody stems). Mix into the butter which is spread over the outside of the trout. Griddle or barbeque for about 4 to 5 minutes each side, basting more with the herb butter. When done the skin will be brown and flesh ready to flake off of the bone.

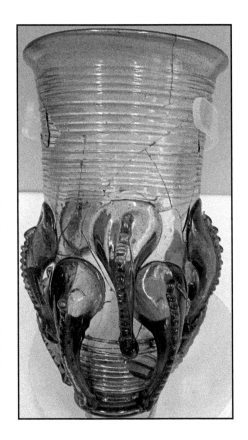

Enjoy the meal with mead drunk from this Anglo-Saxon clawed glass beaker. This beautiful vessel was exceptionally valuable and would have been used by someone of high status. Item: from the Buckinghamshire County Museum Trust collections.

Hare stew with herbs and barley
Rabbits were introduced by the Normans and so not available to Anglo-Saxons (but if hare is not available substitute with rabbit).
50 g (2 oz) butter
1 kg (2 lb) hare
450 g (1 lb) leeks, sliced
4 cloves garlic, chopped
175 g (6oz) pearl barley
900 ml (1½ pints) water
3 tablespoons white wine vinegar
2 bay leaves
Sage (a good handful c. 15 leaves, chopped)

Melt the butter and fry meat to brown with the leeks, adding garlic during the cooking (but do not brown garlic). Add barley, water, vinegar, bay leaves, salt and pepper. Simmer for 1 to 1½ hours until tender, add the sage and continue cooking for 5 minutes, adjust seasoning and serve in a bowl or hollowed out round of crusty bread.

Mutton pottage with mustard

1 kg (2 lb) Mutton, on the bone
1 kg (2lb) any of: onions, carrots (purple variety only), celery, leek, turnip, broad beans
Cooking fat
900 ml (1½ pints) water
Wood sorrel
Mustard

Prepare everything in one large cooking vessel – a large pan to go on the hob today (hanging pot over the fire pit for the Anglo-Saxons). Put the fat in the pan and brown the meat to seal it. Wash and prepare all vegetables, slicing or chunking them, holding the broad beans to one side for the moment. Add sliced vegetables to the pot, with the water. Simmer very gently with the lid on for 1½ hours. Add broad beans, sorrel and mustard simmering for a further 30 minutes.

Serve up with sour dough (a mix of rye, barley and oats) to mop up all the juices. A well baked, firm loaf could be hollowed out as the bowl for the stew, by the time the meat is eaten the stew would have seeped in and softened the loaf.

Curd cheese pastries

225g (8oz) wholemeal shortcrust pastry
225g (8oz) curd cheese
25g (1 oz) chopped stem ginger or crystallized ginger
15 g (½ oz) toasted and chopped pine nuts
Sugar to taste
Lemon juice to taste

Roll the pastry out thinly and cut into rectangles of about 15 x 8 cm (6 x 3 inches). This amount of dough should make 24 rectangles. Bake at 190 °C (Gas 5) for 10 minutes or until brown and crisp. Cool on a rack.
Mix the curd cheese with the ginger and pine nuts, and add sugar and lemon juice to taste. Sandwich two slices of pastry together with the mixture and serve. Delicious!

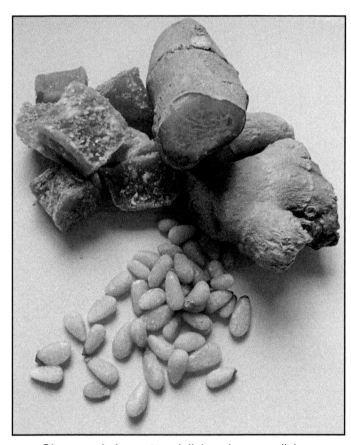

Ginger and pine nuts – delicious in many dishes.

Curd and ginger pastries – simple to make and amazingly good.

10.

Norman peasants to Medieval banquets

Pottages, cabbage, peas, beans, bread and ale for the poor with a vast array of roast meat, stewed venison or wild boar, wild birds, fish, shellfish and piquant sauces embellished with expensive spices for the aristocracy. The fashion for pulverising meat for a variety of dishes such as highly spiced sausage, was a Norman speciality.

Pease pudding hot, pease pudding cold
Pease pudding in the pot, nine days old
Some like it hot, some like it cold
Some like it in the pot nine days old
(or, to be more correct, this dish is called 'pease pottage'!)

Following the Battle of Hastings in 1066 the life-style imposed on the local population by the Norman elite made for a hugely different style of eating for the nobility and the peasants. Land ownership changed dramatically as the Normans put their stamp on the manorial, agricultural, religious and cultural character of the land. Control over local people was such that the land was worked by 'peasants' who were forced to hand over much of their food as payment for using the land. The result was that families were often left with insufficient food. The mills were owned by the landowner who compelled his tenants to use his mill and charged a high toll for grinding the grain for them. Millers became known for their dishonesty – sometimes mixing sand with the flour in order to make a larger profit. Bakers got in on the act and sold underweight loaves. The situation became so bad that it lead to the famous Assize of Bread in 1266 to bring accountability and the law into play, ensuring a fair price for a fair loaf. This law was only changed in 1815 by the Bread Act.

Millstone (above) propped up in a corner as a modern decorative use of this once valuable item for food processing.

Lower stone (left) from a large Medieval pot quern. This is the size of a large car wheel. It is black as it is made from basalt which is an igneous rock and the quern was a common import from either Germany or France in the early Medieval period. Item: from the Buckinghamshire County Museum Trust collections.

Most people had their own small garden where they grew as many vegetables and herbs as they could, and also kept one or more pigs. This source of food was vital to the population, but it is the hardest to gain an insight from archaeology. For the larger gardens insight comes from deeds, wills and Manorial documents. Larger still – the farmers fields provide boundary and ploughing evidence. The rural population worked half-acre strips of land which were close to the village. The population became divided into a hierarchy with freemen renting land and paying in tithes of grain or meat, while the villeynes were forced to work for a certain time each year for the lord of the manor. People had access to areas of common land for each village where they could graze an animal, hunt or trap animals and birds, or collect firewood.

There were great improvements in cultivation methods at this time with advanced types of plough and nailed horseshoes which allowed much more land to fall under cultivation. However, during the 12th century the landowning nobles began to enclose large areas of woodland and common land putting it under private ownership. Severe penalties for poaching were then put in place, with the nobility in charge of the law and enforcing it. If caught poaching, the lower classes could face the death penalty or have their hands cut off. The result was to prevent poorer people from hunting game, not just large animals such as venison or wild boar, but hare, rabbits and wild birds as well. This act alone ensured the diet of the ordinary person became very much poorer, whilst the tables of the nobility groaned under the weight of great quantities of meat. The system could best be described as being run by noble feudal gangsters. By 1217 some of the most strict game laws were repealed which now allowed poor people to hunt rabbit and hare as long as they were only on foot, although they could use dogs.

Only the Lord of the Manor was allowed to have warrens which were provided for breeding the newly introduced rabbit, and only Lords were served a favoured dish of red squirrel. The rabbit, hare and squirrel often went into the stew dishes known as pottages. As well as rabbit warrens, there were dovecots and fish ponds, all becoming common assets for the breeding of animals for food that could be easily harvested and eaten fresh (no need for salting).

The Dovecot at Monks Risborough, Bucks

Besides game, taste was changing for farmed meat. Chickens are relatively easy to rear and so they became more popular with all tiers of society. However, there was a trade-off – hens provide valuable eggs and so would be kept until at the end of their laying ability for poor people. Hence it was the old hens going into the pottages or other dishes. Pullets and capons were for the richer households only. These households would also be able to purchase peacocks, quails, cranes, egrets, bitterns, plovers, woodcocks, pheasants and all game birds.

The previously popular ham and bacon was swapped for a growing taste for beef and mutton. The renowned British breakfast dish of 'eggs and bacon' became a peasant meal by the 14th century, as growing prosperity for the upper classes meant the rich could move on to different foods. The English breakfast as we know it today, with more ingredients, only came about during Victorian times, Mrs Beeton is renowned for her suggestions for this meal.)

The availability of fish was dependant on location – inland towns were dependant on fresh fish from rivers, but coastal towns had much more variety. Monastery records indicate a huge range of fish from today's popular types such as salmon, cod, herring and whitebait to those not so popular today such as lamprey and sea-horse as well as marine mammals such as whale, seals and porpoise. Shellfish were as popular as today, but surprisingly oysters were so abundant that they were food for the poor! Archaeological evidence of bones from sites show a progressive increase in marine fish in the diet, presumably due to better preservation methods, but also due to stricter religious observance of meat-free Fridays.

So, besides the type of meat, what characterised the diets of both the poor and the nobility? The mainstay for the poor was (as always) bread – and one common variety was called maslin made from rye and barley, or a mix of grains including bean (pulse) flour. Archaeologists estimate that about 80% of a farm worker's calories came from grain. Compare that to 40% for higher status people such as Monks. Grain was consumed as ale and pottage as well as the most important – bread. The coarsest breads were eaten by the poor as a mainstay, although it is known that the rich sometimes used a type of flat barley bread (maslin) as a plate known as a trencher! Wheat made the finest flour which, along with the amount of gluten it also contains, made the finest bread with a good rise. To produce the whiter flour it had to be sieved 2 or 3 times through a wool or muslin cloth. The wheat also needed good quality soil to grow. For this reason wheat flour was very expensive. Throughout this period all bread, even the finest, was a brownish colour as all flour had bran – highly refined white flour had not yet been fully developed. The best quality bread was manchet and a luxury loaf called pandemain (panis dominis or Lord's bread). In addition, from the 13th century some bakers were making a kind of French bread produced as rolls and called raise which was enriched with milk, eggs and butter.

Maslin bread – this loaf is a wheat and rye flour mix. A dry coarse loaf, but suitable for mopping up the juices of a pottage.

Considering the importance of bread in the diet it was an absolute tragedy when harvests failed from 1293-95 and again in 1310-12 and 1315-18. This time is referred to as the Great Famine. As this time also saw a plague affecting both sheep and cattle the result was one million people died of starvation. Where peas and beans were available these were used to make bread. *The Annals of Bermondsey* record that people ate anything they could get hold of including cats, dogs, dove dung and even their own children!

When the cattle population recovered cheese was within the means of the poor. Without other methods of preserving milk this was the only way to use any milk surplus. Hedgehog was also on the menu for the poor – they were much more abundant than today. There was a variety of vegetables (as available in previous eras), but also lots of cabbage for the very poor, plus spinach as a new introduction. When the vegetables were added to grain the result could be a thickened pottage. Pottage and bread, along with the staples of the time - peas and beans - were the bulk of the poor diet. A thicker pease pudding was a firm favourite for all tiers of society, served with bacon if the householder could afford to keep a pig.

Spinach a new food for the table and packed full of vitamins and minerals.

Popular Norman spices were introduced to Britain along with garlic, pepper and fennel seed, which were inexpensive, often cooked with shallots, parsley and other herbs to flavour dishes. The nobility could afford (and liked) highly spiced food which would include expensive items such as ginger, saffron, cloves, cinnamon, cumin, mace, anise, caraway and mustard. All these exotic spices were hugely expensive – records in 1418 show 2 lbs of mace cost the same as a cow.

Water was treated with great suspicion at this time as pollution had become a constant health risk. This led to brewing ale becoming as important as baking bread. Records for the Duke of Buckingham's household records 40,000 gallons being consumed in a year! It is often stated that around 8 pints a day was needed for each adult, with weaker ale produced for children. However, ale was relatively expensive and cider could be the option for poorer households.

Left: An early Medieval (13th century) jug with a very personal decoration at the base – indents made by the potter's finger prints. Item: from the Buckinghamshire County Museum Trust collections.

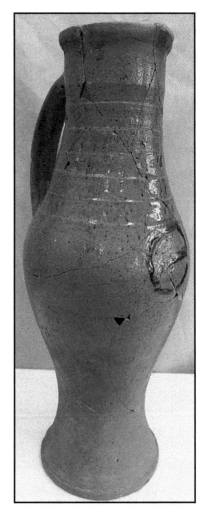

Right: Late Medieval glazed baluster jug from the Brill pottery in Bucks and used for decanting wine or ale. Item: from the Buckinghamshire County Museum Trust collections.

The Normans brought with them some well established culinary skills and recipes. Many of these have stayed with us to the present day - two good examples of Norman dishes still eaten in the 21st century are 'Beef olives' and 'Moules marinières'. Recipes for these can be found in many cookery books today. Culinary prowess was something held in much esteem across the land and cooks were highly valued. The great cooks were so highly prized that they were retained on high wages and even given manorial land. One example of such a reward was that of William the Conqueror's own chef Tezelin who was given Addington Manor in Surrey. Tezelin invented a white bean soup flavoured with dill and another dish of almond chicken called Dillegrout (see below) which was highly praised by William.

The French produced excellent recipe books, but the first English book was written in 1390 called The Forme of Cury. This is a very important book as it contains food facts and information about eating habits plus 196 recipes of the day.

Later on in the Medieval period there were a number of cooks known to have been 'famous' in their day, but many of the surviving manuscripts or recipe books do not have an author. The Boke of Kokery written about 1440 was very likely to have been compiled by a cook from a wealthy house. It contains 182 recipes and many cooking tips including instructing on the art of making a 'custarde'. Unlike today's custard the medieval version was a pie (and originally called 'crustarde' because it had a pastry crust). The pastry lined the dish and it contained meat or fruit covered in a spiced custard (of the type we would recognise as custard - made from eggs and milk).

Whereas the wealthy could eat from silver plates, the poor would eat from wood or horn plates. Everyone had their own knife, and spoons were only rarely used - dishes such as soups would be drunk from cups. Archaeological finds are the only way to know these things and a good example is the cooking pot found on a Buckinghamshire site – the site being a backyard to poor housing in the Norman settlement.

This early Norman pot was found broken and used as packing in a large posthole in Monks Risborough, Bucks (Eyers, 2013). It shows light sooting on the outer surface below the rounded shoulder and it has clearly been used on the fire. There was no limescale on the inner surface, so it was not used for boiling water. It can therefore be assumed that it was a cooking pot, perhaps used for the popular pottages of the day.

Menu for a peasant household
Pease pottage
Broad beans with onions and chunks of pudingis
Unleavened bread or a maslin loaf

Menu for the aristocracy
Dilligrout pottage with manchet bread
Fish blancmange with seasonal vegetables
Lent flan

Norman foody favourites:

Sausages: every era seems to have had its unique love of the sausage. The Normans had three types of sausage: *aundulys*, *saucistres* and *pudingis*. All were made as soon as the animal was slaughtered. The latter was made from the blood, finely chopped onion, chopped fat and spices stuffed into intestine (the black pudding of today). The ingredients for the other two are unknown. There was also a 'white pudding' style of sausage made from pigs liver, cream, white bread and eggs which would be seasoned with items such as raisins, mace, cloves and saffron.

*Norman style black pudding sausages called **pudingis**.*

Aspic dishes: the Normans adored aspic jelly dishes. The aspic is made from boiling pigs' feet, ears and snout with calves' feet and other parts. The resulting liquid was coloured gold with saffron and was poured over a variety of cold cooked meats. When set it could be lavishly decorated.

Pottages were as popular as ever. They could be made from a wide range of ingredients, and eaten by poor and rich alike – the difference being the choice of ingredients. A pottage might be vegetables in season with beans for thickening (cheap to prepare) or it might contain expensive game or fish. Shellfish pottage was particularly high status and was a special treat during Lent when meat would not be eaten. Special assortments of 'pottage herbs' were grown in all gardens. Just like today, many were suitable for drying so their use continued throughout the winter months.

Garlic sauce was popular. The recipe is not known, but the ingredients were: garlic, milk, flour and saffron (so a basic white sauce). It was also noted that it was to be served with goose.

Broad beans and onions. As in Anglo-Saxon times, beans were popular, cheap and readily available. A favourite dish in Richard II's time (c. 1390) was made by gently frying onions in goose fat and adding the cooked beans, frying all until thoroughly cooked and hot. Lavish amounts of parsley were added before serving.

Broad beans in almonds and butter

Ingredients: broad beans, almond milk, butter, breadcrumbs, salt and pepper.

The broad beans should be fresh and young (if larger and older then the skin will need removing after blanching them). Cook the beans in almond milk and a knob of butter (just enough to cover) for about 5 to 10 minutes, depending on their size. Thicken with the breadcrumbs, stirring continuously, season, and serve. A delicious delicate flavour and a really easy way to make a sauce!

Broad beans in almond milk and butter sauce. The almond milk could be made by pulverising the almonds and soaking the mix in milk, the thicker residue can be strained out. Today almond milk is very popular again and readily available.

Maslin bread

This bread was traditionally made with a sourdough starter or sometimes using ale which will activate from the brewer's yeast. The end result will be much closer to the Medieval loaf if a starter dough is used and stone-ground flour. Sometimes this bread would have ground beans as part of the flour mix.

350 g (12 oz) wheat flour
100 g (4 oz) barley flour
200 g (8 oz) rye flour
500 ml warm water
30 g fresh yeast and 1 teaspoon sugar (or 200 g of sourdough starter*)
 1 teaspoon salt
(*if using a starter dough then remember to retain 200 g of dough at the end of the process to keep it going).

Fresh yeast can be mixed with the water and sugar, creaming it with a little of the warm water and then stirring in the remainder of the water. Use this in 5 minutes. Put the salt and flour in a bowl and make a well in the centre. If using fresh yeast then add the activated liquid now; if using a sourdough starter just add the warm water and mix to make the dough – then add the sourdough starter now. Using floured fingers or a wooden spoon mix until you have a sticky dough – add more wholemeal flour if too sticky. Pt the dough on a floured board and knead for 7 minutes to work the gluten and make a better texture when finished. Put back into the floured bowl, cover with a cloth, and leave in a warm place until double in size (around 2 hours). Place back onto the floured board and knead again for 2 or 3 minutes (called 'knocking back'). Make either two round loaves or several smaller rolls. Place on a greased baking tray or baking stone; leave to rise in the warmth for 30 minutes and then put into pre-heated oven at 220°C. After 10 minutes take out and quickly cut a horizontal line around the basal perimeter of the loaves and score the top (just score the top of rolls) and return to the oven at 200°C for a further 40 minutes for a loaf, much less for the rolls, dependant on size. (Photograph above.) A coarse quite heavy, rustic bread. Tasty served with pottage to mop up.

Manchet Bread

To be authentic obtain unbleached stone-ground flour and fresh yeast. The finished loaf should be a round shape. (This recipe has added wholemeal flour to mimic the incomplete refining process of the day as the miller tried to get the whitest flour possible.)

500 g (18 oz) plain white bread flour
200 g (8 oz) wholemeal bread flour
450 ml of <u>warm</u> water
1 teaspoon of salt
Yeast: 30 g (1 oz) fresh yeast with 1 teaspoon sugar (or 15 g (½oz) dried yeast with 1 teaspoon sugar)

Start the yeast – the dried as on the packet using the 450 ml of warm water, and start this usually around 10 minutes before you use it. Fresh yeast can be mixed with the water and sugar, creaming it with a little of the warm water and then stirring in the remainder of the water. Use this in 5 minutes.

Sieve the flour and salt into a large bowl, make a well in the centre with your hand, pour in the activated yeast and gradually combine with the flour to form a sticky dough (add more flour if too sticky). Knead it for 5 minutes on a floured surface. Only add further flour if it becomes too sticky to knead. It should now be soft and elastic.

Put the dough into a floured bowl, cover bowl with a clean cloth and leave in a warm room for 2 to 3 hours or until it has almost doubled in size. On a floured surface knead it for 1 or 2 minutes (called 'knocking back'), shape it into a round and place on a greased baking tray or bakestone (bread tins did not appear until after the 1700s) . Leave for 40 minutes in a warm place to rise. Gently score the top surface with a sharp knife (3 parallel lines or a cross). Preheat the oven to 220°C and bake for 10 minutes before turning the oven down to 200°C for a further 40 minutes. To test if done the base should be golden and make a hollow sound when tapped.
Delicious when eaten warm (use within one day).

Dilligrout pottage

A recipe from William the Conqueror's table prepared by his chef Tezelin. Literally a dish fit for a king. This is a delicious almondy-chicken dish with bursts of flavour from the fennel and a tasty crunch from the toasted almonds.

"Take capouns and seeth hem, thenne take hem up. Take almandes blaunched. grynd hem and alay hem up with the same broth. Cast the mylk in a pot. Waisshe rys and do therto and lat it seeth. Thanne take brawn of Capouns teere it small and do therto. Take white grece sugur and salt and cast therinne. Lat it seeth. Thenne messe it forth and florissh it with aneys in confyt rede other whyt and with almaundes fryed in oyle and serue it forth."

Translations of the more difficult words appear at the end of the book. There are no quantities provided in these early recipes, but it is clearly a thickened white soup with chicken (capons), ground almonds, sugar, salt, pepper and aniseed (fennel) – all very expensive ingredients in Norman times. Here is my recipe for this:

4 chicken breasts (skinless to avoid fat in this delicate soup) parboiled
300 ml (½ pint) water
110 g (4 oz) ground almonds
500 ml almond milk
110 g (4 oz) rice
2 teaspoons sugar
Salt, a good amount, to taste
A generous amount of white pepper
Aniseed confit (I suggest using julienne of one fennel root simmered in sugar & water as a preserve)
Almond slices, lightly fried in oil

Prepare the fennel preserve by preparing julienne strips of a whole fennel root and cooking 50:50 root to sugar and the tiniest drop of water, stirring well. Boil until reduced - to effectively 'marmalade' the root. Put the chicken pieces in a pan with the water and gently boil until partly cooked. Chop into small pieces. Using this liquid add the ground almonds to the pan, then add the milk and rice. Boil stirring occasionally until the grains are thoroughly cooked and soft. Add the chopped chicken, sugar, salt and pepper to taste. Return to the boil. Fry the sliced almonds in a little oil (they will just need a rapid flash with the heat to colour them). Serve the Dilligrout liberally sprinkled with almonds and plenty of shreds of the fennel root, decoratively arranged.

Swan chowder
A recipe from the *Forme of Cury* 1390:

"Chawdoun for Swannes
Take þe lyuer and þe offall of the Swannes & do it to seeþ in gode broth. take it up. take out þe bonys. take & hewe the flesh smale. make a Lyour of crustes of brede & of þe blode of þe Swan ysoden. & do þerto powdour of clowes & of piper & of wyne & salt, & seeþ it & cast þe flessh þerto ihewed. and messe it forth with þe Swan."

Reserve swan blood to one side. Make a broth of the swan including offal by simmering very gently covered in water for 2 hours. Take from the liquid and remove all bones. Chop flesh. Make a paste of bread crusts, the blood of the swan, ground cloves, pepper, some wine, salt using it to thicken and flavour sufficient of the broth to serve with the required amount of meat. Add the swan to the broth re-heat and serve. (NB eating swan is now illegal – this recipe is for interest only!).

Pease pottage
230 g (8 oz) whole or split dried green peas
Water for soaking peas
1.5 litres (2½ pints) water for cooking peas
1 large onion, chopped, and other vegetables may be thrown in too e.g. leeks)
2 large cloves of garlic
Bacon bone with scraps of bacon if possible
Thyme or other herbs
Plenty of pepper
(Salt will only be needed if a bacon bone is not used.)

Place the peas in a bowl and add water to amply cover more than 6 cm above them. Leave overnight for cooking in the morning. Drain peas and discard the water.
Place peas, onion, garlic and bacon bone in a large pot; add the fresh water. Bring to the boil and then turn the heat down to a gentle simmer for 2 hours or until the peas are soft (it may take longer for large whole peas).
Add water if necessary, depending on how long you keep the pot going (Pease pudding nine days old is the rhyme!). Remove the bone and scrape off any meat that might have remained on it. Mix back into the

pottage. Adjust the seasoning. Serve with crusty bread (unleavened or maslin). Peasants who had no bacon bone should be pitied as without a profusion of more vegetables and herbs this would be fairly bland. However, with the bacon cooked on the bone in the pottage it is quite tasty.

Pease Pottage – a dish fit for the peasants.

Lamprey galantine

Henry I (1068 to 1135) was the only English king to have died from something they ate – recorded as dying from a 'surfiet of lampreys'.

The recipe for 'Laumpreys in Galantyne' in the Forme of Cury 1390 instructs:

"Take Laumpreys and sle hem with vynegur oþer with white wyne and salt, scalde hem in water. slyt hem a litel at þer nauel.... and rest a litel at the nauel. take out the guttes at the ende. kepe wele the blode. put the Laumprey on a spyt. roost hym and kepe wel the grece.
grynde raysouns of coraunce. hym up with vyneger. wyne. And crustes of brede. do þerto powdour of gyngur. of galyngale. flour of canel. powdour of clowes, and do þerto raisouns of coraunce hoole. with þe blode and þe grece. seeþ it and salt it, boile it not to stondyng, take up the Laumprey do hym in a chargeour, and lay þe sewe onoward, and serue hym forth."

NB. Not recommended for modern tastes and eels are a protected species: translation: Take the lampreys (eels) and kill them with white wine vinegar and salt; scald them. Cut them open down the mid-line to remove the guts, but reserve the blood. Put the lampreys on a spit (grill or oven) to roast. Retain the fat. Grind the raisins or currants, add some vinegar, wine and breadcrumbs. Add ginger, galyngale, cinnamon, ground cloves. Add some whole raisins or currants to the blood and retained fat, mix and add salt to taste. Add to the lamprey in a serving dish ensure all is piping hot and serve.

Lampreys – eel-like, sinuous, slippery little creatures with sucking mouthparts which cling to other animals in order to suck their blood.

Verde Sawse (Salsa Verde)

The famous, and very popular, green sauce. The original 1390 Forme of Cury recipe for Verde Sawse:

"Take parsel. mynt. garlek. a litul serpell and sawge, a litul canel. gyngur. piper. wyne. brede. vynegur and salt grynde it smal with safroun & messe it forth."

Take parsley, mint, garlic, a little wild thyme and sage, a little cinnamon, ginger, pepper, wine, bread crumbs, vinegar and salt. Grind it in a pestle and mortar (or use liquidiser) add a touch of saffron. It is ready to serve with meat or poultry. Use lots of parsley, but take care with the mint and sage. The bread is only there to thicken and bind – so not too much. The rest is all down to taste preferences. Delicious and goes well with pork or chicken.

Peacock and partridge with ginger

This dish is popular in the C15th, but the original 1390 Forme of Cury recipe is very short and simple:

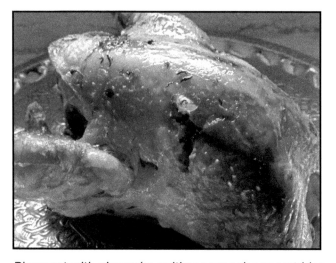

Pheasant with ginger (as neither peacock nor partridge were available at the time of recipe testing).

"Pecokys and Partrigchis schul ben yparboyld and lardyd and etyn with gyngenyr."

Choose partridge or pheasant for this dish – parboil the birds. Remove, drain and pat dry to remove excess water. Rub lard all over the birds. Place slices or parings of ginger inside the birds. Roast until cooked. Use the ginger liquid to add to stock or wine and reduce to form a jus, pour over the birds and serve with seasonal vegetables. (We used pheasant as this was available at the time – served with just the ginger parings from inside the bird. It would be equally delicious served with a ginger sauce.

Fish blancmange

The name 'blancmange' for this recipe simply means 'white food', and originally all the term meant. Today the word is used for the cold wobbly dessert. The original recipe says:

"For to make blomanger of fysch.
Tak a pound of rys les hem wel and wasch and seth tyl they breste and lat hem kele and do ther'to mylk of to pound of Almandys nym the Perche or the Lopuster and boyle yt and kest sugur and salt also ther'to and serve yt forth."

Basically this is a recipe for a white sauce made with rice cooked in almond milk which is seasoned with sugar and salt and poured over the boiled/poached fish. This dish has a very delicate flavour and benefits from chopped dill being sprinkled over it before serving.

Egerdouce of Fysshe (Sole in sweet-sour sauce)
A recipe from the *Forme of Cury* 1390. Other white fish can be used instead of sole.

"Take lochs or roches other tenches other soles; smyte hem on pecys. Fry hem in oyle. Take half wyne, half vinegar, and sugur, and make a sirup; do therto oynnouns icorue, raisouns couraunce, and grete raysouns. Do thereto hole spices, gode powdours and salt; messe the fyssh and lay the sewe above and serve forth."

The fish should be fillets and fried in oil. Make the sauce by gently softening the finely chopped onion in oil. Make a syrup with sugar/honey in half red wine and much less than half red wine vinegar (so as not to make it too acidic). Add to the onions and add raisins, currants and sultanas, bring to the boil and simmer until reduced. Add flavourful spices and salt to taste (ginger, mace and ground pepper are suggested). Simmer for a round 10 to 15 minutes. Pulverise with a mortar until smooth (or cheat and use liquidiser!). Arrange the fish on a serving dish, pour the sauce over and serve forth!

This is a classic sweet and sour sauce. The traditional recipe is too acid due to the large amount of vinegar for modern tastes – so go sparingly as you can always add more, but you cannot take it away.

Doucettes
"Take porke & hakke it smal, & eyroun y-melleyd to-gederys, & a lytel milke, & melle hem to-gederys with hony & pepir, & bake hem in a cofyn, & serue forth."

Shortcrust pastry to line a 20 to 25 cm pie dish, or several small ones
450 g (1 lb) Pork, cooked and chopped into small pieces
3 Eggs, beaten
Milk, a glug
1 teaspoon runny honey
Pepper, a generous quantity
Salt enough to season to taste
Make the shortcrust and line the pie dish(es), allow to rest and then bake blind. Chop the pre-cooked pork into small pieces (using roast pork is possibly best). Combine the meat with the beaten eggs and a little milk (only enough to make it a thick, spoon-able mix). Season the mixture with the honey, pepper and salt. Place this filling into the pie dish(es) and bake until the filling has set. This is a very tasty dish.

Lent flan
"For to make flownys in lente.
Tak god Flowr and mak a Past and tak god mylk of Almandys and flowr of rys other amydoun and boyle hem togeder' that they be wel chariaud wan yt is boylid thykke take yt up and ley yt on a feyr' bord so that yt be cold and wan the Cofyns ben makyd tak a party of and do upon the coffyns and kerf hem in Schiveris and do hem in god mylk of Almandys and Figys and Datys and kerf yt in fowr partyis and do yt to bake and serve yt forth."

Make a pastry crust and cook a flan case (baking blind in the oven). Make a thick custard with rice flour (use cornflour) and almond milk, add sugar to sweeten. Allow to get cold. Fill the flan case by arranging figs (if fresh figs then coat in a little icing sugar) and dates (both cut into quarters or halves) in the almost cooked pastry case. Pour over the almond custard and cook until set. [Cofyns in the original recipe above is a lovely word for pastry case!]

We found it a shame to cover the lovely fruit arrangement with the almond custard – so next time we will cook the pastry completely, and then place the custard in the tart case first and set it. Then purchase ready to eat dates and figs arranging these over the top of the custard. Very tasty.

Lent flan – before cooking with fruit laid out and after cooking with the almond custard poured over, as per the original recipe.

Pine nut tarts

Chestnut pastry (a basic shortcrust made with chestnut flour) and pinch of saffron for colour
Filling: crushed pine nuts, honey, wine, ground ginger and cloves.

Make pastry cases, leave to rest and bake blind. Place all the filling ingredients into a pan and boil until a syrup forms. Remove the cloves. Fill the pastry cases and bake.

Colouring the white dishes

White dishes were very popular (many having a basis of milk or almond milk) but they could be coloured by a wide variety of items. For instance carrot peel would produce a deep blue (all carrots were purple at this time), parsley was often used for green, yellow from saffron, and pink came from rose petals or bloodwort root. Banquets were the places to show off a multi-coloured spectacular!

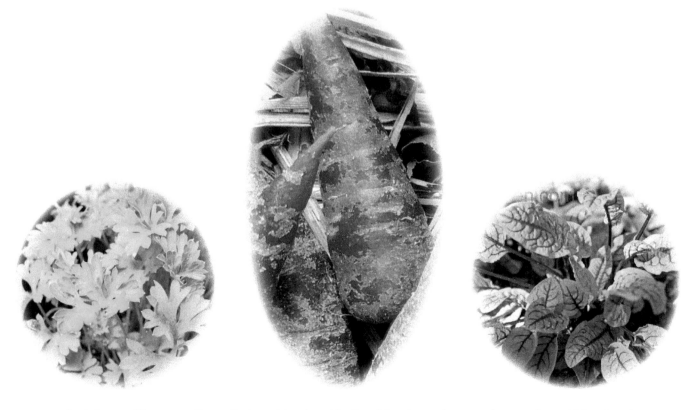

Just three of the many items that could colour Medieval food: parsley, purple carrots and bloodwort

11.

Tudor treats – plus pies, potatoes and hops

Tables filled with food, often no separate courses - just all placed out with a spread of spit-roasts, brown trout, chicken, many types of pie, mushy peas, salads and a wealth of green vegetables in butter. Cooking with cream and citrus became very fashionable – all finished off with sweet treats such as suckets and marchpane. A true passion for sugar had started!

> Sing a song of sixpence, a pocket full of rye
> Four and twenty blackbirds baked in a pie
> When the pie was opened, the birds began to sing
> Wasn't that a dainty dish to set before the king?

The influences on food during Tudor times came largely from new discoveries during exploration by seafarers, but also on inflation with large unemployment. The latter two problems were blamed wholeheartedly on Spanish conquests flooding the market with their 'ill-gotten' gold. However, history would show the British navy to have played some part in this activity themselves.

There are several Tudor cookbooks available such as A proper new booke of cookerye (1545), *Delightes for ladies* (1602) written by Sir Hugh Plat which includes a lot of sweet dishes, and a series of culinary and medical books by Gervase Markham (1615) called *The English Huswife*.

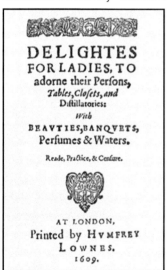

The title page of Delightes for ladies 1609 – a very popular book of the day.

Of all the famous dishes of the day it is the pies that are the outstanding dish of Tudor times. They could be very simple and homely pies made with economical cuts of meat or vegetables, or they might be elaborate and time-consuming masterpieces suitable for an elegant table. To eat humble pie is a saying coming from this era as 'the humbles' or 'umbles' were the offal parts of an animal such as liver and heart; such a pie would only be given to those lower down the social order. Different styles of pie might be served at one end of the table – with good cuts for the high status end, while the lower end ate the umbles. If you were of a higher status and you were given a piece of the umbles, then this would be intended to insult you! A wealthy dinner table would certainly have a pie served containing top cuts of meat – large pies could contain a whole side of venison, but needed massive ovens to bake them! This might be one of the reasons the brick oven started with the Tudors. The decoration of the pie crust was very elaborate; they can be seen in paintings with intricate patterns of decoration such as lacework or heraldry.

Whatever they contained, the pie was a very clever invention as the pastry (originally called 'paste') acted both as a container for food and helped to preserve the contents for much longer than otherwise would be possible. The first pastry contained no fat at all. This fat-free pastry was not actually for eating, as the resulting crust was very hard and tough. The juices would be drained out of the meat pie at the end of cooking through a hole made in the crust before baking. Clarified butter would then be poured in, which sealed the contents from the air. Pies prepared this way could last for weeks. When ready to serve, the pie could be re-heated (a fresh spiced gravy could be added at this point if wanted) and taken to the table where the crust would be split open to reveal the steaming, tasty contents. The pie was the 'show off' item on the table. This dish evolved over the Tudor period, and by the end of the 16th century the pie crust had fats such as butter or suet added, and sometimes egg, all of which made it less hard and edible along with the contents. These totally edible pies were highly prized items and were often given as gifts.

The Tudor kitchen at Hampton Court. A large brick-built fire-place able to accommodate a large spit-roast and multiple other dishes.

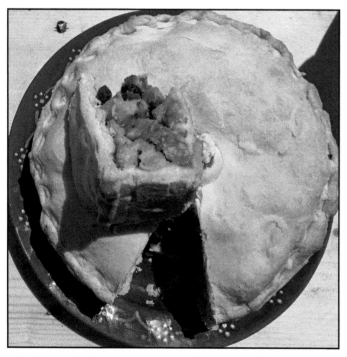

Sweet potato pie. This simple pie for modest incomes could be made with marrow and flavoured (if you could afford them) with dates, raisins, cinnamon and mace - with a touch of sugar, of course.

Despite the rise of popularity in the pie, the spit roast remained a really popular method of cooking. The art of trussing the meat and securing to the spit with tapes, skewers and guiding spikes had been perfected a long time before. The task of turning the spit was a dreadful job as it involved both dreadfully high heat one side, but cold on the person's other side. It was also very hard work – turning was required for hours during the roasting. The job was therefore given to the lowest of people who were called the 'turnspit'. Calling someone a turnspit was later to become a term of abuse. However, in 1536 Dr Caius reported the use of a 'spit dog' for the purpose. The dog ran within a 1 metre diameter wooden treadmill which was linked to an iron axle via a pulley and to the spit by a second pulley. The dog simply ran for hours in the wheel to turn the spit. Little short-legged dogs were specially bred for the purpose. It is said that if they did not run fast enough a few of the hot embers would be placed within their wheels – encouraging a faster pace so as not to get burnt feet. Clearly this was a long time before the RSPCA!

In contrast, the basic food for those on meagre incomes was based around those items which could be easily grown in household gardens, or foraged for locally. The poor would source all produce locally. This would include bread, fish if caught in a local stream and a variety of local vegetables such as carrots, cabbages, peas , onions and herbs – hence pottage and pease pudding would form a large part of the poor diet. At the coast there would be different varieties of fish and shellfish available.

A Tudor feast. Lucas van Valckenborch, late 16th century.

However, for those with more wealth, dining was also about showing off. Some items held great status. Surprisingly (when compared to today) young chicken was a sheer luxury product. Chickens were kept for their eggs and so they were a very expensive luxury to eat as a poultry dish before the bird had finished laying. The dining table could be filled with meat dishes such as spit-roast wild boar, venison or peacock and a variety of pies. A famous Christmas speciality was wild boar brawn. Another Christmas delicacy fit for royalty was the much-loved lamprey-pie. The eel-like, sucker-mouthed lampreys were much sought after and could cost as much as 5 shillings each. Fish remained as popular as ever, but the Tudors especially enjoyed a fish blancmange. The first blancmanges were all savoury, not sweet as we have become used to today.

Spices were a very important 'show off' item. Cinnamon sticks were worth a small fortune, as was pepper, ginger, nutmeg, saffron, cloves, mace and a host of other exotic spices. Sweet treats were another very special and expensive item - a bag of sugar would cost about £300 in today's prices. Sweet dishes such as Marchpane (marzipan) made with ground almonds, sugar and a little rosewater was especially popular. Preparing and grinding the almonds was very hard, time-consuming work. This is where the status in food lay – the more labour intensive a dish was, the higher the prestige the household gained by its presentation. All food was beautifully decorated and it was known that very fine dining could incorporate decoration in gold leaf.

Fine dining for the Tudors
A sample menu from *A Proper Newe Booke of Cookerye* 1560

The whole selection would be flamboyantly brought in by servants, with guests watching in anticipation of the feast to come - the dishes laid out all together on one large groaning table.

Jellye
Peacooke — Sauce wyne and salt
Two connies or half a dosyn rabets
Sauce mustarde and suger
Half a dosyn chekyns upon sorell soppes
Half a dosyn pigeons
Mallarde
Teyle — Sauce mustarde
Guiles — and verges
Storke
Heronshewe. —
Crane — Sauce galentyne.
Curlew
Bitture
Bustarde
Fesande — Sauce water and salt with onyons slyced

Continued . . .

Halfe a dosen woodcocks - Sauce mustarde and suger
Halfe a dosen partriches
Half a dosen tayles - Sauced as the fesantes.
A dosen of Quayles
A dyshe of Larkes
Two pasties of redde deare in a dyshe
Flummery
Tarte
Trifle
Gensbread
Fritteris

The Tudor kitchen for a wealthy household would always have a male cook in charge – women were relegated to menial tasks like water carrying, pounding and grinding. Women were in charge of minding the charcoal

fuelled stoves – the carbon monoxide given off was known to make cooks faint or even kill them!

Charcoal oven at Hampton Court – toxic gasses sufficient to make cooks collapse or die! Cooking vessels were held in slots over the heat.

Women would also be in charge of bread-making. This was an important commodity in any household, rich or poor, it was just the quality of the flour that would vary – with the finest and whitest being the most expensive. However, without yeast the preparation of any loaf was tricky and it was making it light that was the skill. Getting it to rise was an art. A clever tactic was devised whereby the bread dough could be placed under an apple tree to rise. Clearly the unknown science behind this idea being that the dough would take in some of the natural yeasts which are at high levels around apples. Ale could be used as well, added to the dough for its yeast content and flavour.

The Milk Maid. Johannes Vermeer 1658-1660. Also showing a variety of bread.
https://commons.wikimedia.org/w/index.php?curid=13408941

Herbs were important in the kitchen, not only for culinary uses, but also for medicinal purposes. They were also used for counteracting smells and for cleaning. A vast array of herbs would be grown in formal gardens, often walled gardens, to allow a more protected environment and prolonged growth as well as attractive walking areas. A good description of a vast number of food and herbal remedies can be found in John Gerard's 1597 book *Herball or Generall Historie of Plantes*. His book became required reading for botanical students of the day, with information on sources of plants from his travels, and herbal remedies. His recommendation for ground pepper to cure sight problems is dubious "All pepper ... cleanseth the dimness of sight." Despite many of his remedies being very incorrect and often misguided (appearing humorous today) it did lead to a great interest in natural ways to cure illness and keep healthy. One amusing line for a love potion recipe reads: "Sow-bread when beaten up and made into little flat cakes, acts as an amorous medicine to make one in love if eaten".

The walled garden at Greys Court, Oxfordshire (National Trust). A Tudor Garden re-designed in the 19th century as a beautiful place to walk, as well as being functional.

In the kitchen many jobs for the household were very labour intensive, but had to be maintained on a daily or regular basis in order to keep the family or household fed. Every day jobs would include dough making and baking, brewing ale, butter-churning, cheese-pressing, garden produce growing, tending and harvesting, salting meat, making preserves, not to mention all the chopping, meat preparation, grinding and blending that would be needed to prepare dishes. The preparation would be on a central large table with an open fire range with a multitude of pots, pans, knives and other implements.

A dramatic change to eating habits came with Henry VIII's dissolution of the monasteries. In one fell swoop this led to the demise of fishponds which were a mainstay of the Monk's diet and essential for fasting days. In 1541 Henry decreed that fasting days could now include new items to the diet such as eggs, cheese and milk. But despite Henry's break with the church, the traditional fish days continued to be observed. Indeed during Elizabeth's reign Wednesdays and Saturdays were pronounced fish days. More days were subsequently added, resulting in what was called 'Political Lent' when more than half the days of the year were fish days! The underlying idea behind this dietary restriction was to support the fishing industry, so ensuring lots of coastal habitation and lots of seamen. Queen Mary later restored the fast day on Fridays only and fish was again the recommended option, but not enforced by law. Without the fish ponds, and with a growing dislike for the taste of 'muddy' river fish, pickled herrings became the mainstay for many households on Friday. Fish and chips eaten on Friday night are still very common in Britain, now becoming a treat more than a religious necessity.

A contribution to dietary change was also provided by Queen Elizabeth I as explorers to the newly discovered Americas brought back a variety of produce such as maize, kidney beans, the Turkey, potatoes and sweet potatoes, pumpkins, red and green peppers, globe artichokes, French beans and aubergines and tomatoes - all introduced by 1570. However, it seems that all these introductions received a great deal of mistrust. They were not thought of as good food value, many being largely ignored for some considerable time and some were believed to make you ill. Potatoes were not considered as 'healthy' as they were found underground. The sweet potato was the first variety to be known and used in Tudor cookery (see the recipe below). Today's 'ordinary' variety of potato was introduced later and was called the Irish Potato for some time. At first, these were thought of as suitable food only for pigs and peasants. On the whole, the new food introductions were treated with great suspicion.

However, one introduction that was very popular was vanilla – which was believed to be an antidote to poison. Another introduction that found full approval was the introduction of hops from Flanders in 1525. Although brewers were at first sceptical of adding the hops to the mash, the flavour of the product was highly appreciated by the drinkers! By the end of the century it was beer (which is ale with hops) that became the nation's drink.

However, without doubt, the most popular food introduction, and the one that has undoubtedly done more harm to health than any other, albeit the most adored – was sugar! This was such an expensive luxury that is was only available in small quantities. It was stored in locked caddies and was transported in locked vehicles. The cost was due to the labour intensive work needed to process and clarify the final product from the imported sugar cones. Sugar confectioners were paid very well – at least three times that of labourers. But it was thought well worth it for the pure delight of the taste, but also for the 'health giving' properties that were being attributed to it. As examples sugar coated coriander seeds were eaten as a digestive, candied roses could cure gonorrhoea, it gave energy and vitality, believed to act as natural Viagra.

For the first time cookery books began to aim at more ordinary households, with books such as A proper newe booke of cookerye, printed in 1560, being aimed at ordinary householders and not just the chefs of the big houses. However, it remained as true as always that, for the poor, little meat if any formed part of the normal menu. Bacon or pork was the only likely meat to be affordable by those on low incomes. Coloppes and egges (bacon and eggs) remained a firm favourite from previous eras. Just like today, it was now common to have three meals a day: a light breakfast of cold food, dinner was the name of the midday meal, and the evening meal (taken anytime between 5 and 8 pm) was supper. Meals would be eaten from wooden trenchers and bowls or from pewter plates. Drinks such as beer, ale, wine or fresh water (the latter only safe from the well) were drunk from pottery or wooden vessels, although pewter and silver cups are known from rich households. Cutlery was now the 'full set' of knife, two-pronged fork and a spoon – with guests often bringing their own set to the meal!

Some typical dishes of the day would involve mutton (often with pearl barley to add substance and to thicken), pies, herring, salmon, lemon sole, trout, bacon or oysters. The 'brown' meats such as beef or venison were more expensive and so tended to be for the richer households. The most common way to cook meat and poultry was by 'seething' (boiling) – the flavours enhanced with the addition of a very wide range of spices and herbs. Desserts were a Tudor weakness and the sweet dish would be on show as the table-centre. Fruit such as figs, gooseberries or pears were very popular but the newly introduced citrus fruits, such as oranges, were particularly enjoyed as sugar coated desserts. With no other method of keeping food fresh, a lot of produce was salted, pickled or preserved in sugar.

Fruit – the sweeter the fruit, the more it was enjoyed.

Figs – fresh or more often preserved – a sweet treat.

Here follows a flavoursome range of dishes from Tudor times.

Tudor raised pork pie
Raised pie pastry:
220 g (8 oz) flour, 1 teaspoon salt, 70 g (2½ oz) lard or dripping; about 280 ml (½ pint) water.
Pie ingredients:
450 g (1 lb) pork

1 teaspoon salt; ¼ teaspoon pepper
Pinch of dried sage or finely chopped fresh leaf
2 tablespoons stock
A little egg and milk to glaze
When cooked:
70 ml (⅛ pint) jellied stock (70 ml/ 1/8 pint stock with ¾ teaspoon gelatine)

Prepare the pie ingredients first as the pastry must be used while still warm. Cut the pork into very small pieces or mince it. Mix with the other ingredients for the filling.

Make the pastry by putting the water and lard into a pan, heating until the water boils, then stir in the flour and salt, mixing lightly until smooth. Take ¾ of the pastry to line a pie case. Fill tightly with the meat mixture.

Roll out the lid to slightly larger than the top of the case, wet the edges of the pastry placing the lid on and sealing it well. Crimp the edges and decorate lavishly with any shaped off-cuts of pastry – little leaves or other decoration. Stick them down with egg wash. Make a whole in the centre of the lid, brush with egg wash. Bake for 10 to 20 minutes at 230 °C until just beginning to brown, then reduce the heat, cover the top with paper, and allow to cook gently at 180 °C until the meat is cooked – about 2½ hours.

Leave to cool. When cold pour in the jellied stock through the hole, which should be on the point of setting when added. Delicious – better than any pie you could buy! The small pies shown here take a shorter cooking time of course – dependant on their size.

Tudor raised pork pies. Here a simple crimped decoration, but these could be decorated very elaborately. These were often filled with a variety of meat, any juices poured out and then melted butter poured in the hole. Our recipe used the jellied version.

Mistress Duffeld's capon with orenges

2 kg chicken portions
50 g (2 oz) butter
A little flour seasoned with salt and pepper
150 ml (5 fl oz) stock (the recipe is for marrow-bone stock, or substitute with chicken stock)
270 ml (9 fl oz) orange juice
90 ml (3 fl oz) white wine
3 teaspoons candied orange peel
1 pinch each of: rosemary, ginger, mace and cinnamon
1 teaspoon sugar
225 g (8 oz) prunes (stones removed)
50 g (2 oz) currants
6 slices of manchet bread toasted (see recipe Chapter 10)
1 orange thinly sliced

Melt the butter in a large pan (suitable to take the whole quantity for slow cooking on the hob. A casserole dish could be used in the oven if preferred). Coat the chicken portions with the flour and fry gently until lightly brown. Add all other ingredients to the pan, mixing very well as they are added. Fit a tight lid to the pan/dish. Simmer very gently for about 1 hour if on the hob, longer in the oven. Check the seasoning. To serve: place chicken portions on the toast, pour over some of the broth, decorate with the orange slices and serve. Enough for 6 people.

To make the best Dressed Salmon

A recipe from Sir Kenelm Digby (1827) *The Closet…*
"An excellent way of dressing Fish. Take a piece of fresh Salmon, and wash it clean in a little Vinegar and water, and let it lie a while in it, then put it into a great Pipkin with a cover, and put to it some six spoonfuls of water and four of Vinegar, and as much of white-wine, a good deal of Salt a handful of sweet herbs, a little white Sorrel, a few Cloves, a little stick of Cinamon, a little Mace; put all these in a Pipkin close, and set it in a Kettle of seething water, and there let it stew three hours. You may do Carps, Eeles, Trouts, &c. this way, and they Tast also to your mind."

Sweet potatoes in rose and orange syrupe

A recipe from Elinor Fettiplace's *Receipt Book* **(1605):**
"Boile your roots in faire water until they bee somewhat tender then pill of the skinne, then make your syrupe, weying to every pound of roots a pound of sugar and a quarter of a pint of faire water, & as much of rose water, & the juice of three or fowre oranges, then boile the syrupe, & boile them till they bee throughlie soaked in the syrupe, before you take it from the fire, put in a little musk and amber greece."

1 kg (2 lb) sweet potatoes
½ cup sugar
¼ cup water and rose water 50:50
Juice of 3 oranges
Vanilla extract (a drop in place of the musk and ambergris, which is a waxy substance secreted by sperm whales).

Make the syrup by adding the sugar to the water, rosewater and orange juice mixture. Boil to reduce it to syrup add a drop of vanilla extract. Cook the sweet potatoes in water until tender, skin them and slice. Pour over the syrup and serve. This has a nice subtle flavour, but very sweet for modern tastes (even though potato to sugar was 1:1 in the original recipe – so hugely sweeter still!).

Lady Kent's syllabub

A recipe from Sir Kenelm Digby (1827) *The Closet…* Tudor syllabubs were rather different to the syllabub we know today – which is largely a type made from whipped cream which is a form common from the 1700s. The milk or milk/cream mix was warmed and then poured from a height into the alcohol or other flavouring such as lemon juice and sugar as below. Sometimes this might be milk fresh from the cow's udder into the syllabub pot. A frothy drink (not curdled) would be the art and only the best housewife could do it!

To make the ledy kents silebub
scald a quart of cram and a quart of milk with sum mace and nutmeg cut in to it with a litell lemon pile then take it of and stir it untell it is but as hot as milk for the cow then put half sak and helf whit win with a litel jus of lemon and suger file your silebub pote helf full with it then power your cram very hie into it this is best to be mayd the day befor you eat it …

Crystallised fruit – Tudor suckets

A recipe from Gervase Markham (1615) *The English Hus-wife:*
"Dissolve sugar…in rosewater. Boile it to an Height. Put in your roots, fruits or flowers, the sirrop being cold. Then rest a little, after take them out, and boild the sirrop again. Then put in more roots. Then boyle the sirrop the third time to an hardnesse, putting in more Sugar, but not rose-water. Put in the roots, and let them stand until they candy."

There were wet suckets served as tasty treats, or the dry suckets were easily made by taking the preserved items from the syrup and drying out. Roots could be parsnip or carrot; flowers could be any edible flowers: violet, rose, borage, rosemary – anything in season, with stamens removed and any bulky calyx removed.

The recipe for fruit suckets was chosen:

450 g (1lb) fruit: grapes, cherries, small plums, damsons, oranges, apricots, etc
180 g (6 oz) sugar (for first boiling)
400 g (14 oz) for subsequent boiling.
Water (some rosewater could be added as per the original recipe above)

Select only perfect, ripe but firm, fruit. The best result is achieved by only making each crystallised fruit separately as each will take different cooking times and interfere with individual flavours. Apricots, plums and damsons should be pricked but left whole. Remove pips from grapes. Cherries need the stone removed. Larger fruit such as pears, oranges and pineapple need to be peeled and cut into smaller pieces.

Place in a large pan, cover with water and simmer until just tender, but still perfectly intact. Using a straining spoon gently lift fruit out of the pan and lay it out in a heatproof dish. Measure out about 300 ml (½ pint) and use this to mix with the first sugar for boiling. Bring to the boil stirring continuously and then pour this over the fruit ensuring it is all covered in syrup. Leave for 24 hours.
Drain the syrup off the fruit (using a colander or sieve). Put the fruit back into the dish, add 50 g (2oz) more of sugar. Bring to the boil again, pour over the fruit again and leave for 24 hours.
Repeat three more times continuing to use a further 50 g (2 oz) sugar each time.

Now drain the syrup off once more into a large pan and add 75 g (3oz) sugar, bring to the boil, add the fruit to the pan and simmer for 3 minutes. Place back in the heatproof dish and now leave 48 hours. Repeat with more sugar to achieve thick syrup which resembles the consistency of runny honey. If too thin, then repeat with more sugar and boil again.

Now add the fruit to the thick syrup, simmer 3 minutes, leave to cool and sit in the syrup for 4 days.
Take fruit from the syrup and leave to drain by suspending on a raised rack. They will drip dry, sticky at first, but then dry. They can be dipped in castor sugar for a light coating which is very attractive. Serve as a sweet Tudor treat.

Tudor mixed fruit, cherries, dates, almonds and crystallised ginger – firm favourites in many recipes both sweet and savoury.

Lavender shortbread

225g (8oz) flour
2 tablespoons lavender flowers, finely chopped
140 g (5oz) butter
80g sugar (caster)
2 small egg yolks
Pinch salt   Makes about 24 biscuits

Put the softened butter and the lavender into a mixing bowl and beat together to get the best flavour from the lavender. Cream the sugar & salt into the butter, beat in the egg yolks, and then stir in the flour, working together sufficiently to form a smooth paste.

Roll out to about 4 mm (⅛ of an inch) thick or less, cut into the required shapes and bake at 180 °C for about 10 minutes (dependant on thickness).
Pre-heat the oven to 160 °C/Fan 140 °C (Gas 3). Cut each "sausage" into about 10 slices and put them on the prepared baking trays, allowing a little room for them to spread. Bake for 15 to 20 minutes, until the biscuits are pale golden brown at the edges. Lift them off the trays with a fish slice or palette knife and leave on a wire rack to cool completely.

Gooseberry fool

A recipe from Sir Kenelm Digby (1827) *The Closet…*

"To make the best Gooseberry Fool
Take your Gooseberries, and put them in a Silver or Earthen Pot, and set it in a Skillet of boyling Water, and when
they are coddled enough strain them, then make them hot again, when they are scalding hot, beat them very well
with a good piece of fresh butter, Rose-water and Sugar, and put in the yolke of two or three Eggs; you may put
Rose-water into them, and so stir it altogether, and serve it to the Table when it is cold."

Marigold tart

A recipe from *A proper newe booke of cokerye* around 1570.

"To make short Paest for Tarte: Take fyn floure and a cursey of fayre water and a dish of swete butter and a lyttel
saffron, and the yolkes of two egges and make ti thynne and as tender as ye maye.
To Make a Tarte of Marigoldes, Prymroses or Couslips: Take the floures and perboyle them tender, then strayne them
with the yolkes of three or foure egges, and swete curdes, or els take three or foure apples and perboyle withal and
strayne them with swete butter and a little mace and bake it."

This is an easy dish to make – simply a standard shortcrust pastry (half fat to flour) using butter and some
saffron and 2 egg yolks to make a wonderful yellow coloured pastry. Bake blind. For the filling parboil 3
tablespoons of Marigold petals. Cream together fromage frais, egg yolks, 1 tablespoon flour and 1 tablespoon
caster sugar, and the flavouring. Whisk the 2 egg whites and gently fold into the mixture. (Mace is suggested
in the original recipe, but orange zest and juice is a lovely flavour.) Stir in the drained marigold petals, fill the
flan case and bake in a hot oven for around 30 minutes when it will be firm to touch.

A marigold. Today an unusual ingredient for food,
but in Tudor times eating flowers of many types was
very common. This tart could also be used for borage
flowers – a Roman introduction to Britain and it is one
of the flowers that pops up in salads and a Pimms
cocktail today! It has a very gentle cucumber flavour.

Marchpane cake
This would often be the centre-piece of the meal or banquet. Marchpane (marzipan) was exceptionally
popular.
450 g (1 lb) ground almonds
225 g (8oz) castor sugar
2 tablespoons rose water
Glaze: 1 tablespoon rose water and 2 tablespoons icing sugar

Mix the almonds, sugar and rose water together to make a paste. Knead it to ensure it is completely smooth.
Leave a small amount to one side for decoration (about a tenth?). Roll the rest on greaseproof paper to make
a round of about 7 to 8 mm thick, ensuring the edges are neat. Bake in a cool oven on a baking sheet (150°C;
gas 3) for only 15 minutes. Take out for 15 minutes and return to the oven again. Repeat the process of in
and out of the oven to ensure the marzipan dries, but is only very lightly coloured.

Make the glaze by mixing the remaining rose water with the icing sugar. This will be thin and can be brushed over the marchpane for the final return to the oven – which will be only 5 or 10 minutes this time until dry and glossy. Remove and cool. Decorate with the marchpane that was set aside which can be rolled and cut into shapes, or made into animals or flowers as preferred. Sugared confectionary was sometimes added as well. The gold leaf decoration was for the Royal Court who could afford it!

Pastry

Pastry came in several forms for main course pies or flans for dessert. This enriched pastry is coloured with saffron. A pastry recipe from A proper newe booke of cookerye:

To make short paest for tarte
Take fyne floure and a cursey of fayre water and a dysche of swete butter and a lyttel saffron, and the yolckes of two egges and make it thynne and as tender as ye maye.

Use the pastry to line a flan dish and fill with a multitude of fruit of choice: strawberries into a cooked flan case or figs, pears, apples, cherries, or a combination, cooked in the flan case and finished with a sugar glaze. More recipes may be found on-line using the recipe book titles or the authors' names above in the search terms.

12.

The Stuarts – suet puds, seafood and sweets

An austere period, but seafood became very popular (as it was cheap). Sweet things were highly sought after, as was the new idea of the boiled suet pudding. Another new idea – the fork – came into play and eating with your fingers became frowned on.

The Stuart period 1603 to 1714 saw turmoil in the country as civil war erupted, plague swept the country and the great fire of London took its toll. There were religious tensions, an execution of a king and a republic formed. The austere life-style developing during this period could be partly blamed on the fact that, for ordinary people, food constituted 80% of their income. Puritans believed you earned your place in heaven by working hard and pointless frivolities such as celebrations and feasting were frowned upon. Cromwell banned feasting at Christmas – replacing the festivities with fasting days instead!

However, by the close of the period the slave trade feeding the colonies and the West Indies with a free workforce brought huge profits to the British companies involved in developing new plantations and trading in sugar and spices. Sugar although hugely expensive was very popular with the rich, who wanted many sweet puddings and sugar in their tea and coffee. A spin off was that this resulted in a good trade in silver sugar spoons, boxes and tongs. Despite exotic new fruits being imported such as pineapples and bananas, these were regarded as being poisonous and treated with mistrust like many other fresh fruit. The result was that food remained mostly simple fare.

A Greybeard jug also known as a 'Bellarmine jug'. In the 16th to 17th century wine and beer were drawn from barrels into salt-glazed stoneware jugs. The image is said to be of Cardinal Robert Bellarmine (1542-1621). He was a fierce anti-reformationist and it was common for Protestants who disliked him to smash the jugs! Item: from the Buckinghamshire County Museum Trust collections.

This era saw the dawning of one simple new idea – which remains a British favourite today. This was to make a dough 'crust' and fill it with sweet or savoury items, wrapping it in a boiling cloth, and then either boiling or steaming it. Simple and instantly popular, the suet pud has remained on British dinner tables from its first record in Cambridge University in 1617 to the present-day. Nobody quite makes a pudding like the British! The suet and flour version became most popular, but puddings could also be made from oats or barley flour. The Scottish developed the same idea and called them 'clootie dumplings'. Although simple to make and a rustic type dish, it was popular with all classes. It should be noted that boiled puddings were made before this date, but the method was to put the sweet or the savoury meat filling into a sheep stomach or similar body part and boil that.

The pottage remained a good staple favourite and in 1656 William Cole revealed the popular additions to this dish when he said:

"With the buds of elders, nettle tops, watercresses and alexanders,
good women use to make pottage with in the Spring time."

Watercress harvested from a local chalk stream for a 'good woman' to make a pottage as in the quote above.

Nettle tops were commonly used as a spring tonic and this was still being practiced in the 'nettle tea' popular in the 1930s. Nettles are now seeing a modern revival being used today in soups, teas and as a vegetable (it tastes a little like spinach).

New items were added to the diet, or at least 'rediscovered' and under intense cultivation. In particular these were mushrooms and the cauliflower, with truffles re-delighting the dinner table. Little almond macaroons became popular and, in contrast, so did very large cakes - some reputedly up to 20 pounds in weight! The wonderfully named 'posset' was enjoyed for centuries since Stuart times, although overtaken in Georgian times by the syllabub (which is more creamy and thick). The posset started life as a warming drink which gave rise to Shakespeare's Lady Macbeth poisoning Duncan's guards with "drugg'd possets'.

A posset pot dating to 1661. Spoon out the top two creamy layers and drink the boozy bottom layer through the spout. http://wellcomeimages.org/indexplus/image/ L0057146.html

The Stuart form of posset was made from milk curdled with alcohol or citrus juice. Sack posset, with Spanish fortified sherry-style wine, was particularly popular in the 15th and 16th centuries. They even perfumed them with musk and ambergris (ox and whale secretions respectively). Posset is therefore similar to the Tudor syllabub – simply re-named and changed slightly. Poorer people made possets with ale and thickened them with bread - a bread thickened posset of this kind survived into the 1950s in the English Lake District - it was called Fig Sue. A well made posset had three layers. The uppermost, known as 'the grace' was a snowy aerated foam. In the middle was a smooth spicy custard and at the bottom a pungent alcoholic liquid. The grace and the custard were enthusiastically consumed as 'spoonmeat' and the sack-rich liquid below drunk through the 'pipe' or spout of the posset pot.

Mrs Cromwell's recipes were published in 1664 by Randal Taylor. The publication showed examples of her recipes and was actually aimed at shaming her by displaying her poor skills and penny-pinching ways. This attempt to blacken the Cromwell name has misfired over time, as it is now the only record of actual first-hand recipes used in this era, and specifically those eaten in this famous household.

Following this, in 1709, T. Hall published his book The Queen's Royal Cookery. It is one of a flurry of books published at this time which revealed secrets of the royal kitchen – a subject which fascinated the public. In this case, Queen Anne was the focus of much gossip and people wished to emulate the lifestyle or simply be informed of what she ate or liked. It is a wonderful book due to lots of illustrations of a busy kitchen with pastry being kneaded, dough being made, cooks actively turning spits and more. Some of this is available to read from the British Library website.

A Stuart menu

Choose from the following popular dishes to get two courses – starter and main, or main and dessert:

First course
Barley broth
Roast tongues
Buttered scrambled eggs
Tansy eggs (eggs & cream flavoured with tansy)
Boiled teats (cow's udders)

Second course
Boiled venison, goose or rabbit
Boiled crab
Salmon or trout
Pike in red wine and anchovy sauce

Scotch collops of veal or beef
Beef in the Italian style
Hog liver pudding
Chicken with asparagus
Roast swan or heron
Potatoes and boiled seasonal vegetables
Grand sallet (a fancy salad which could include eggs and poultry)
Spiced spinach tarte

Dessert
Egg custard
Bread and butter pudding
Almond cream pudding
Syllabub

Cow's udder – an item in Stuart and Georgian recipe books, but a food never mentioned in modern kitchens. It appears most often as a starter course in Stuart menus.

My Lord of Carlisle's Sack Posset
A recipe from Sir Kenelm Digby *The Closet* (London: 1671)

"Take a pottle of Cream, and boil in it a little whole Cinnamon, and three or four flakes of Mace. To this proportion of Cream put in eighteen yolks of eggs, and eight of the whites; a pint of Sack; beat your eggs very well, and then mingle them with your Sack. Put in three quarters of a pound of Sugar into the Wine and Eggs, with a Nutmeg grated, and a little beaten Cinnamon; set the Bason on the fire with the Wine and Eggs, and let it be hot. Then put in the Cream boiling from the fire, pour it on high, but stir it not; cover it with a dish, and when it is settlede, strew on the top a little fine Sugar mingled with three grains of Ambergreece, and one grain of Musk, and serve it up."
[Use vanilla extract instead of ambergris and musk.]

Mrs Cromwell's Scotch Collops of veal
1 fillet of veal
8 eggs
Salt, grated nutmeg
Handful of thyme, leaves stripped off stalks
110 g (4 oz) capers, finely chopped
3 anchovies
½ pint oysters
450 g (1lb) sausages
Butter for frying
Cup white wine
Cup of water
Splash of vinegar with chopped lemon, pat of butter
¼ finely chopped lemon
Slices of toast or fried bread

Take a fillet of veal and cut it into broad but thin slices. Beat 8 eggs with a little salt and nutmeg. Partly fry the veal in the butter before adding the sausages and oysters. Blend anchovies with a little wine, adding the water and then the eggs and capers. Pour all into the pan over the veal and oysters stirring continuously. Add the pat of butter, vinegar and lemon. Keep stirring so the result is smooth and not curdled. Adjust seasoning and serve with 'sippets' (small slices of toast or fried bread).

Offal dishes
Mrs Cromwell made use of many types of offal. There are numerous recipes for brawn, stewed udders and tongues, liver pudding (using the 'guts'), marrow pudding (eaten at breakfast), and marrow bones with ambergris. Other economy dishes include dressed cod heads, boiled perch and eel pie. The ingredients for these are either not able to be sourced today or often not to our taste. The following recipes are rather nice though.

Game dishes
Mrs Cromwell offered numerous recipes for these such as roasted leveret, stewed duck (where onions, anchovies and lemons were the main sauce flavouring), pigeon pie, rabbit hash, fried rabbit and rabbit with oyster. Oysters feature a lot at this time as they were so cheap and they were used to 'pad out' the dish so as to use less of the expensive meat.

To stew a fillet of beef in the Italian fashion
1 fillet of beef, flatter is better for the marinade, ensure any sinew is removed
Wine for the marinade
Pepper and salt to season
'Tamara' *
Beef stock
A few whole cloves and mace (if put in a muslin pouch then it is easier to retrieve at the end)

(*Tamara is the name for a popular blend of spice made in bulk and stored in an airtight container:
2 oz coriander seed, 1 oz aniseed, 1 oz fennel seed, 2 oz cloves, 1 oz cinnamon with a little winter savoury
- all ground in a pestle and mortar.)

Place the beef in a dish with enough wine to cover it, adding pepper, salt and a tablespoon of Tamara. Work it into the meat. Placing a weight on the meat keep it covered in the fridge to marinade (Mrs Cromwell says for 2 nights and 1 day). Transfer the meat only to a pipkin (a small pot or pan) and cover with a good beef stock, add the whole cloves and mace, placing it over a low heat with a tight lid. Mrs Cromwell says 'cook it till it be enough'. Very low on a modern cooker top was fine in just over an hour; an oven will take longer. This would be perfect for a modern slow cooker for the same 'Cromwellian' result. The meat was amazingly tender. Remove the whole cloves and mace, serve the beef with a generous amount of broth spooned over it. Delicious.

Skinke pottage

Leg of beef, cut into 3 portions = 3 'knuckles'
A pottle of water (2 litres or 4 pints in today's money!)
A few cloves, mace and whole pepper (if tied in a muslin pouch is easier to remove)
A 'bundle' of herbs: sweet marjoram, parsley, rosemary, thyme, sage, winter savoury
Salt
3 large (whole) onions
3 marrow bones
Oatmeal or wholemeal bread (Manchet) enough to thicken the broth
Ground saffron
Thick slices of bread (Mrs Cromwell says both French bread and wholemeal, Manchet)

Boil the beef in the water with the cloves, mace and pepper. Skim the pan before adding salt to season with the whole onions and the herbs tied into one bundle. Simmer gently, the time is dependant on the size of the meat portions. About one hour before serving add the marrow bones and add either the ground oatmeal or the wholemeal bread (maslin or manchet) to thicken. Shortly before serving add the saffron, bring to the boil and serve by placing the marrow bones on large, thick slices of French bread arranged around the beef in the centre of a large dish. Arrange further slices of Manchet toast around the edge of the serving dish. A hearty, hot dish.

Mrs Cromwell's chicken with asparagus

Sometimes nothing changes – this dish was popular with the Romans too!

1 whole capon or chicken
Ample salted water for boiling
Mace, parsley, butter
Sippets of bread (*sippets* are finely sliced or cubed toasted or fried bread)
Asparagus, 2 bundles
Butter, melted to serve

Put the mace, parsley and butter inside the chicken. Boil/simmer in the salted water until fully cooked. When almost ready to serve boil the asparagus, prepare the *sippets* by toasting or frying as preferred, and melt a little butter in another pan. Place the sippets on a large serving dish, place the whole chicken carefully on top of these, spoon over some of the broth, arrange the asparagus over the chicken and pour over the butter. Serve immediately whilst piping hot.

Mrs Cromwell's hog liver suet pudding

Rose water was often used by cooks, instead of water, as it was safer.

450 g (1 lb) hog's liver, boiled then grated
Bread (quantity just more than the liver)
Flour (same quantity as the liver)
6 eggs
225 g (½ lb) beef suet
225 g (½lb) currants
A good glug of rosewater
A good quantity of nutmeg, mace, cinnamon, ginger and cloves all ground
Milk and cream
Hog guts (Mrs Cromwell suggests cooking this mix in sewn up guts. For modern tastes and availability

it might be best to use a traditional suet crust pastry and thinly lining a pudding bowl to be filled with the liver mixture.)

Boil the liver, grate it and mix with a greater quantity of breadcrumbs. Mix in the flour, eggs, beef suet, currants and the rosewater along with the spices and as much milk or cream as needed to make a thick batter consistency. Line a large pudding basin with suet crust and fill with the mixture. Seal with suet crust lid. Wrap in greaseproof and steam the pudding for a couple of hours. This is a stodgy, very filling dish with a strange texture. The combination of the spicy and sweet flavours are a little odd for the modern palate, but nice and very different!

To stew a dish of trouts

Mrs Cromwell's recipe:

"Let your frying pan be very hot with clarified butter, then split them in two and give them a sudden brown with a forcible heat, and let a stewing dish be ready prepared with gravy, oyster liquor, a little claret wine and vinegar. Fry three or four sliced onions, and when they are brown put them to the fish, with a handful of parsley fried green, a sliced nutmeg, two or three anchovies, and let it just boil up together. Then dish up your trouts upon sippets: notwithstanding the best way for crispness and sight of your fish is to fry the split fish, as trout and salmon, very crisp and brown: dish it up with the inside uppermost."

Spiced spinach tarte

A recipe from Elizabeth Birkett 1699:

"Take a good quantity of spinage and boyle it, and when tis boyled, put it into a Cullander, that the water may run out from it, then shred it very small, and season it with a good flow of sugar, and a pretty quantity of melted butter, then put in the yolks of eggs, and beat them altogether. Then make a sheet paste very thin, and put it upon a dish, so put your Tarte stuff upon it, then another sheet to cover it."

Spinach tarts were very popular in this era and could have lots of spices and dried fruit added to them as well.

Mrs Cromwell's pear pie

Pears, peeled but whole
Water
Sugar
Shortcrust pastry dough

Bake the pears in the oven with a little water and lots of sugar, in a sealed oven dish, for only about 15 minutes to start the softening. Put to one side to get cold, reserving some liquor. In the meantime make a shortcrust pastry dough (use half fat to flour in the recipe and make enough for the quantity of pears). Line a high sided pastry pie dish (called a coffyn in those days!). Place the pears still whole in this pastry-lined dish, adding some cloves and whole cinnamon with sugar and a little of the liquor they were cooked in – and so bake it!

To make puffs (spiced meringues)

Another recipe from Elizabeth Birkett, 1699, for an early type of meringue which is more like a biscuit. They could also have ground almonds added.

"Take a pound of double refined sugar, beat and sift it fine, then take 2 graynes of Amber Greece finely beaten, and mix it with the sugar, and then take the White of the egges and beat it till it be all a froth. So put your sugar by degrees, and beat it as you would do Biskett, then take a pretty quantity of coriander or Carrowayes, put them in And roll it up in little Balls about the bigness of a Nutmegg and lay it upon Wafers and set them around like Loaves and bake them."

The ingredients from above are: 4 egg whites, 250 g (8 oz) caster sugar, 10 ml (2 teaspoons) ground coriander or caraway seed. Vanilla extract can be substituted for ambergris.

The puffs need to be baked on a greased non-stick tin or greased paper and need a very cool oven of around 130 °C (Gas mark ½ to 1) for about an hour – they will be a light beige colour when ready. Crisp, light and very tasty.

13.

Fancy dining Georgian style

Fancy dining with beautifully laid out tables. Two or three courses and multiple dishes served in each course. The first course: soup and small savoury dishes; the main course: a roast, fish or a game pie with side dishes of fancy vegetables; the dessert course: a great variety of milk puddings, syllabubs, fruit dishes or pastries. Cakes were very popular, but a touch heavy to our tastes.

Austerity of the Stuarts turned to opulence, extravagance and precision for the Georgians. The era saw the first of four Georges and William IV and it was a boom time with developing factories, urbanisation and a growing population. Large families were common-place in Georgian times. If the family was poor then the woman of the house needed to be 'canny' with the dishes she cooked to make the most of cheaper ingredients sourced from their own garden or very locally, with many extras coming from the nearby woodland. The housekeeper of a richer household would be able to source a greater variety of produce and serve many dishes for each course in rather opulent style. Recipe books of the time would not only show the ingredients and methods, but dictated exactly how it should be presented and where to place the dish on the table!

Books relating to kitchen organisation include the very popular Eliza Smith's 1739 *The Compleat Housewife* and *The Ladies Companion* printed 1753; M. Bradley 1756 *The British Housewife*; A. Chambers 1800 *The Ladies Best Companion*; and A. Beauvilliers 1814 *L'Art du Cuisinier*. William Kitchener was a Regency cook and he developed a 'magazine of tastes' which was literally a box containing a wonderful array of flavoursome items to add to dishes. His recipes were published in *The Cooks Oracle*. He also launched a supper club called 'The Committee of Taste' whose members met to eat the delights he prepared.

Many recipes books were published by ex-housekeepers (dedicated to their previous employer). 'Foodies' with books famous in their time were William Verral (landlord of the White Hart Inn of Lewes in Sussex), Professor Richard Bradley (Prof of Botany at Cambridge who collected recipes and wrote the *Lady's Director*) and Elizabeth Raffald a business woman who opened the first domestic agency in Manchester (as well as bringing up her thirteen daughters!). Her book was exceptionally popular and remained so for a very long time – Queen Victoria later copied sections of it into her diary.

As for previous eras, the recipe ingredients can often be tricky to source today. Items such as leverets, widgeon, heron, a calf's head and a cow's udder are rarely stocked by your supermarket or even the local butcher. Other ingredients such as swan are illegal to kill and eat, and we would probably not want to follow Eliza Smith's recipe for pickled sparrows! If some unusual ingredients cannot be sourced from specialised ethnic stores (for instance Afro-Caribbean and Asian stores), then some of the recipes below will need suitable alternatives!

It was also still commonplace to observe a fasting day (a Church of England custom) and hence housekeepers also needed to plan a variety of dishes which would serve this purpose. The main rule was that they should have no meat or stock in the dish and Eliza Smith's soup recipe is a good example.

There is a wealth of information on eating habits from the vast number of cookbooks. It is clear that the rye and barley breads were out of fashion, but the enriched and well-fruited and spiced bread became highly prized, along with cake.

Changing animal rearing practices ensured a good supply of meat all year and meat played a much larger role in the diet than the previous Stuart era. Beef, sheep and pigs were the most numerous. There was a vast change in fish eating habits as the compulsory fish-eating days eventually came to an end. River fish immediately went out of fashion, with the exception of salmon and trout. Previous fish ponds were transformed into ornamental lakes. Sea fish was difficult to obtain away from the coast, but was still popular when available. Fish was potted, salted, pickled and dried to enable it to be transported inland. Vegetables such as broccoli, asparagus, globe artichokes and mushrooms blossomed in popularity. A range of vegetables could be produced along with a wide variety of fruit in walled gardens.

The real 'show off' ingredient – an exotic pineapple. When placed in pride of place as the table centre this really showed your guests you had wealth, buildings, knowledge and staff that could cater for these tropical plants that would take two years to grow and ripen.

The food snobbery of the large houses led to building of orangery and pineapple houses along with ways of growing climate sensitive fruit such as peaches, nectarines, melons and grapes. Dairy food was very important with large quantities of butter and cream going into fancy dishes.

Wine was very expensive and so only for wealthy households. However, this was a time for very cheap brandy and gin and the Georgian era developed the well known reputation for a vast consumption of alcohol. Gin drinking in particular caused so many deaths and untold misery that some writers of the day proclaimed their fears on the stability of British social structure. The government were forced to raise taxes on spirits to try to curb the trend. Ale drinking remained as popular as ever.

Beer and water from wells was safe to drink, with milk often being drunk as syllabubs. Cider was largely consumed in the counties that produced it. Tea became so popular that special tea gardens were opened for the public (the first one in Vauxhall, London). Chocolate and coffee became the breakfast drink. Coffee also became very fashionable and coffee houses were opened in many towns. However, these coffee houses were only used by men – women would never dare to enter them, which would be deemed shameful, as it was felt they should entertain friends at home.

A Georgian tea bowl. The earliest tea gardens and tea sets featured tiny handless cups in deep saucers. Milk and sugar was served with it in the traditional way and teaspoons became essential. Item: from the Buckinghamshire County Museum Trust collections.

Right: Sketch of a Georgian coffee house. These ladies do not look as if they are worrying about their reputation! Photo: Sally Lunn's collection.

Salt-glazed stoneware drinking mug which was popular between 1700 and 1800 and often with personal names or a motto on them. The decorative item here is an angel. Item: from the Buckinghamshire County Museum Trust collections.

Below: The front parlour laid for a simple lunch. A reconstruction at the New Inn at Stowe (National Trust).

The kitchen at the New Inn, Stowe (National Trust). Kitchen innovations included built-in charcoal ranges and stoves – the open hearths began to get closed up during the 18th century.

The faggot kitchen at Sally Lunn's in Bath, part of the kitchen museum and eating house. The oven used faggots of wood to bake a variety of bread and buns.

A Georgian menu

Select from the following for two or three delicious courses:

Starter

Asparagus soup
Green pea soup
Salomongundy

Main course

Fricasée of chicken
Beef steaks with parsley sauce or anchovy sauce
Hare Collops
Calve's Head pie
Leg of mutton
Haunch of roast venison
Ragou of mushrooms
Artichokes
New potatoes

Desserts

Chocolate cream
Blancmange
Lemon Jelly
Compote of apricots
Apricot tart
Orange tart
Fruit – melon, peaches, greengages

First courses:

Eliza Smith's fasting day soup

150 g (6 oz) of spinach (or if sorrel is available use half spinach:sorrel)
Parsley, a good handful chopped
Half a small lettuce, chopped
25 g (1 oz) butter
1 onion into which 15 cloves have been inserted
40 g (1.5 oz) fresh brown breadcrumbs
1.5 litres (2.5 pints) water and 90 ml (3 fl oz) white wine
3 egg yolks
Juice of 1 lemon
40 g (1.5 oz) pistachio nuts, chopped finely
Salt and pepper to taste

Wash and chop the spinach (and sorrel too if used) and get all ingredients ready. Melt the butter in a large pan. Add the spinach, sorrel, parsley and lettuce for 5 minutes until very wilted. Add the cloved onion, breadcrumbs, water, salt and pepper. Simmer for 20 minutes. Remove the onion and puree the soup - we can liquidise, the Georgian housekeeper would have to pass it through a coarse sieve. The liquidised soup may still need to be passed through the sieve to remove larger 'bits' and ensure a smooth texture. Whisk the egg yolks with the wine, lemon and nuts and then whisk them into the soup which has been returned to the pan. Cook gently for a few minutes while stirring continuously (do NOT boil!) and when thickened adjust seasoning and serve. Serves 6.

Salomongundy

A very popular hors d'oeuvre which comprised a number of small tasters displayed in tiny dishes on one large presentation platter. It could contain all sorts of dishes which contrasted in flavours or blandness and sweetness or tartness. It was also a way of using up the left overs!
Compare this to the Victorian 'Salmagundy'.

Examples of what to put in little ramekin dishes:

Flavoursome: anchovies, herring, a selection of pickles, boiled onions (preferably small and whole); a sharp oil and vinegar dressing
Bland items:

- cooked meat selection (chicken, veal, pork, pigeon or any other available);
- cooked white fish (any available)
- salad items such as finely sliced celery, cucumber, etc
- artichoke hearts
- raw mushrooms
- finely sliced lettuce
- a selection of soft cheese

Present attractively on a large platter for your guests to select and dress.

A small and simple Salomongundy: bread, gherkins, mussels, artichoke hearts, sliced cucumber, anchovies, smoked mackerel fillets and slices of ham.

Main courses:

Eliza Smith's Salmon Pye

750 g (1.5 lb) fresh salmon (the cheaper tail, or for modern times a large tin might be used!)
1 lemon, sliced
450 ml (15 fl oz) water
450 ml (15fl oz) white wine
Bunch of mixed fresh herbs, as in season
Salt and pepper to taste
325 g (6oz) of both white flour and wholemeal flour
60 g (2.5 oz) of both butter and lard
3 hard-boiled egg yolks
9 anchovies, chopped together with 1 tablespoon oil reserved from the tin
100 g (4 oz) mussels or oysters, chopped (frozen works well)
50 g (2 oz) fresh brown breadcrumbs
50 g (2 oz) soft butter
Pinch nutmeg and pepper
Handful of parsley, sage and thyme

Put the salmon (if using fresh) in a pan with the lemon slices, water, wine, herbs and seasoning. Simmer for 15 minutes until the salmon is cooked. Remove the salmon, putting the liquid to one side.
Meanwhile make the pastry by rubbing the butter and lard into the mixed flours with enough cold water to make soft dough. Use two thirds to line a 20-25 cm (9 inch) cake tin (loose bottomed type is easier to remove the cooked pie, but you can line the tin with foil which helps to remove it). Set aside to rest.
Mash the hard-boiled egg yolks, mix with the anchovies, mussels and/or oysters, breadcrumbs, soft butter, anchovy oil, herbs, and pepper. Form small balls with the mixture which the Georgians (and Victorians after them) called 'forcemeat'.

Fill the pastry base with the salmon, placing the forcemeat balls here and there into the mixture. Cover with the remaining third of pastry. Make a hole to pour in some juices later. Bake in a moderate oven (190°C or 375°F or Gas 5) for 30 to 35 minutes until the pastry is cooked through and golden.

Strain and reheat the cooking juices and pour about 120 ml (4 fl oz) into the hole in the pastry lid (if using tinned salmon then concoct a suitable 'juice' with tin liquor, lemon juice and oil plus herbs and seasoning, to make a delicious moistening addition to the pie).

Serve hot, but just as nice cold. Serves 6.

Stew'd beef steaks
A recipe from Prof Bradley that he collected after sampling the dish at the famous Spring Gardens in Vauxhall, London. Delicious and serves 6.

6 thin steaks suitable for frying
2 slices streaky bacon, finely chopped
2 onions, finely chopped
Peel of 1 lemon
3 anchovy fillets
5 cloves
Large bunch of fresh herbs (mixed such as parsley, thyme, sage and bay leaves)
3 tablespoon red wine vinegar
300 ml (10fl oz) water
Salt and pepper to taste
25 g (1 oz) butter
25 g (1oz) flour

Place the steaks in a suitable heavy-based pan or casserole dish and add all ingredients except for the butter and flour. Simmer gently on the hob or in the oven for 20 to 30 minutes until cooked and tender. Remove the steaks from the liquid and dry with kitchen towelling. Pass the liquid through a coarse sieve to remove all the floating ingredients which can now be discarded. Coat the steaks in the flour. Melt the butter in a frying pan and fry the steaks until golden and even slightly crisp. Place on a heating serving dish. Add the rest of the flour to the butter to make a roux, cook it through for a couple of minutes before taking off the heat and gradually add the cooking liquid. Bring to a simmer, stirring for a couple of minutes until it thickens slightly. Adjust seasoning, pour over the steaks and serve immediately with a side dish of vegetables.

Vegetable side dishes:

Stewed cucumbers
Another recipe from Prof Bradley, this one comes from the Devil's Tavern in Fleet Street, London.
Unusual texture, but tasty and surprisingly nice! Cooked cucumbers in a variety of guises were very popular with the Georgians.

2 large cucumbers, sliced thickly (no need to peel)
4 medium onions, finely chopped
300 ml (10 fl oz) light red wine
2 tablespoon seasoned flour
50 g (2 oz) butter
180 ml (6 fl oz) water

Place the cucumber, onion and 60 ml (2 fl oz) red wine into a pan. Place on the lid and simmer very gently for 10 minutes, stirring occasionally. Drain and dry the cucumber and onion mix with kitchen towelling. Toss them in the well seasoned flour. Melt the butter in a frying pan and fry the cucumber and onion until beginning to colour. Slowly add the remainder of the wine and the water, stirring constantly whilst bringing to a simmer for a few minutes to thicken the sauce. Check the seasoning and serve. The texture is a little weird for modern taste. Serves 6.

Desserts:

Lemon syllabub

The nature of a syllabub (similar to Stuart Possets) is to have a spoonable flavoured froth on the top of the glass, through which the flavoured wine mix is drunk from beneath. This recipe is adapted to suit modern lifestyles as the original Georgian syllabub often instructed the cook to use milk 'direct from the cow' as the very act of milking produced the desired froth of a syllabub! Lady's who wished to prepare the syllabub in their kitchen would whisk it with birch twigs.

2 lemons, rind peeled into thin strips, and the juice
300 ml (10 fl oz) medium to slightly sweet white wine
Sherry or brandy, optional, can be added to the wine for more of a 'kick'
1 tablespoon sugar
300 ml (10 fl oz) whipping cream
Nutmeg, freshly grated

Put the lemon rind into the wine and infuse for several hours; then remove the rind. Put the sugar, lemon juice and cream into a bowl and whisk (electric whisk recommended as birch twigs are hard work!). Pour the syllabub into glasses and leave for several hours, after which time the frothy cream part will have separated from the flavoured wine part. Delicious. Serves 6

(Modern guests will probably not understand Georgian syllabub, so make sure you explain that the concept is to spoon the top, and then drink the bottom contents of the glass – or they may just think you are a terrible cook!).

Orange tart

This deliciously zesty tart topped with crispy peaks of meringue is reputed to have been a favourite of Queen Charlotte.

Shortcrust pastry (100g, 4 oz or enough to line the tart tin)
2 large juicy oranges
75 g (3 oz) butter
75 g (3 oz) castor sugar
 3 egg yolks and 1 white
Vanilla essence
2 egg whites and 50 g (2 oz) caster sugar for the meringue

Make the pastry, line the tin and bake blind.
Make the filling by grating the zest from the oranges and put to one side with the juice of the oranges. Cream the butter and sugar very well and beat each of the three egg yolks in separately, add 2 tablespoons of orange juice along with the rind and vanilla essence. Whisk the single egg white until slightly stiff and fold into the orange mixture. Fill the cooled tart case. Whisk the remaining 2 egg whites with the sugar to make a 'soft

peak' meringue. Pile it onto the filling forming little peaks. Bake in a moderate oven for 15 to 20 minutes. Makes one medium size tart. Zesty and delicious.

Mrs Raffald's rich caraway seed cake

For the traditional recipe use the wholemeal flour, but if you prefer a lighter cake use the modern fine white flour. This is a traditional cake served to farm labourers to celebrate 'seedtime' – when the last grain had been sown in the fields.

225 g (8 oz) wholemeal (or white) flour
225 g (8 oz) butter or margarine
225 g (8 oz) castor sugar
4 eggs, separated
25 g (1 oz) caraway seeds
1 level teaspoon *both* of cinnamon and ground nutmeg

Beat together the butter (or margarine) and sugar until light, and add the egg yolks, caraway seeds and spices, mixing well. Whisk the egg whites until fluffy and just holding a peak and fold them gently into the mixture, also adding the flour. Grease and line a cake tin (a loose bottomed one is best) place the mixture in it and bake for about 1 hour at 180°C (350°F). When cooked a test skewer will come out clean. Allow to completely cool before cutting.

Mrs Raffald's rich caraway seed cake. If you like caraway then you will love this cake. Caraway seeds were added liberally to this popular cake and other dishes – it is thought as a medicinal agent as it was reported as aiding digestion and it would combat flatulence!

Mrs Raffald's grapes in brandy

This is an after dinner treat to be served with coffee.
450 g (1 lb) white seedless grapes
100 g (4 oz) sugar
300 ml (10 fl oz) cheap brandy

Remove all stalks from the grapes and reject any that are bruised or damaged. Place in a preserving jar (or two depending on the size) along with equal amounts of the sugar and brandy. Close the jar and leave for about 4 weeks. Serve in an elegant crystal bowl with cocktail sticks to spear them.
(Note the brandy/sugar juice may be re-used for the next batch, just add a little more sugar.)

William Verral's Recurrant Jelly Fritters

William's 1759 recipe is simple and gives no defined quantities, but he says there are several sorts, and it is easy to improvise for a tasty treat. Fritters of many types were very popular with the Georgians.

Rich pastry
Redcurrant jelly
Lard for frying
Icing sugar

Make a good rich pastry. Take small amounts of the pastry and roll out very thinly. Brush all over with beaten egg and place a teaspoon of redcurrant jelly centrally. Cover with a second thin layer of pastry and press firmly all around the edges to seal it firmly so that none of the jelly will escape. Put some lard in a pan, and when very hot fry the pastries until golden. Shake over the top with icing sugar and serve.

Chocolate cream

"Take a pint of good cream, and heaped spoonful of chocolate scraped, put it in when the cream boyls, stir them well together, beat the yolk of 2 eggs and stir into it the cream, sweeten it to your tast, let the Eggs have a boyl or two to thicken it put it into a Cholcolate pot and Mill it, so hold the Pot high and pour it into a dish."

175 g (6oz) of plain chocolate will be needed for 150 ml (¼ pint) double cream. Use a bain-marie and take the dish off the heat to add the egg yolks. A couple of drops of vanilla essence will intensify the flavour.
Only one word is suitable here – wow!

Sally Lunn

This was a very popular (brioche-style) bun often served for a Georgian breakfast. The recipe was that of a Huguenot refugee called Solange Luyon . She had fled and settled down in Bath finding work in a bakery in Lilliput Lane. There is now a tearoom on the location of the bakery (the lane now called North Parade Passage) and they specialise in making Sally Lunn buns.

3 tablespoon butter
350g (12 oz) plain flour
1 tablespoon dried active baking yeast
225ml milk
2 eggs
3 tablespoon caster sugar
1/2 teaspoon salt

Mix together half of the flour and the yeast in a bowl and put to one side.

Put the milk, sugar, butter and salt in a saucepan and heat to warm through and melt the butter. Add this mixture to the flour. Add the eggs. Beat vigorously to mix thoroughly (cheat with an electric mixer if your arm is not strong, as you need to keep it up for 2 minutes!)

Start adding the remaining flour with a spoon at first and then as it becomes stiffer, by hand to form dough. Knead the dough until smooth. Cover with a damp cloth and leave in a warm place until double in size (about 1 hour).

Knead the dough again (knocking back) divide the dough into equal portions and form the bun shapes - placing them on a greased tray. Cover again and leave in the warm until risen to twice the size again (about 45 minutes).

Bake in a hot oven (190°C or Gas 5) until cooked (about 10 minutes). To test just tap them on the bottom and they will sound hollow.

Once baked tear open and eat with lashings of butter.

A Sally Lunn bun at Sally Lunn's in Bath.

14.

Victorian recipes – designed to delight

 Sumptuous and for the lady of the house to show off her skills. A medley of new kitchen inventions helped the task in hand.

Cleanliness is the most essential ingredient in the art of cooking:
A dirty kitchen being a disgrace to mistress and maid.

Above Anne Cobbett 1851 *The English Housekeeper*
and from Mrs Beeton:

I have always thought that there is no more fruitful source of family discontent than a housewife's badly-cooked dinners and untidy ways.

As for all the previous eras, food and its preparation in Victorian Britain displayed many facets. The style, produce and equipment used for cooking depended almost in entirety on the wealth of the household. For those falling within the lower income range simply continuing to put meals on the table was a major battle. For the middle incomes simple food could be lavishly presented. The large affluent country houses used eating as a social pastime and aimed to 'show off' their status by preparing sumptuous dishes for guests at dinner parties and by designing lavish ways of displaying expensive exotic ingredients. Above all, they purchased a range of new equipment to make this easier.

Books of the time informing households of the 'how to do it' for household organisation and dining include: E Hammond's 1826 *Modern domestic cookery* and M. Holland 's 1843 The complete economical cook. For recipes and advice you cannot get better than Mrs Beeton's Book of Household Management 1861. However, there was a wealth of cookery books giving full and detailed advice such as Mrs Marshall's Cookery Book; Eliza Acton's 1845 *Modern Cookery*; Mrs Harriet A. de Salis's set of books called *A la Mode* and Kettner's 1877 *Book of the Table*.

Title page of Mrs Beeton's Book of Household Management 1861. The female role was very well-defined during the Victorian period. In short, it was all about making the man of the house happy, well fed and comfortable. This concept was well supported by full advice in books such as Mrs Beeton's on how to play this role. The upper class woman was not expected to cook of course, but to manage her staff that did all the work for the family.

A select of dishes from Mrs Beeton's book showing the housewife how food should be served.

"Cookery and the artificial preparation of food has one chief object i.e. to assist in the wonderful series of changes known as digestion and assimilation"

Mrs Beeton 1909

Quotes such as this from Mrs Beeton show the dichotomy flowing through ideas surrounding food. On the one had there is the plain, matter-of-fact scientific approach of Mrs Beeton with simple food being linked to good health. Then on the other hand the idea of producing the most sumptuous, elegant and time-consuming dishes that were more to show off talent and wealth to those being entertained than considering their health. There is also the conflict of reality versus ideals as Mrs Beeton's strong advice for quality, meticulous standards in preparation and serving is in stark contrast to the large quantity of diseased meat being sold. Sausages frequently secretly contained horseflesh and tales such as Sweeny Todd told all kinds of terrible items in shop-bought pies! This problem was made public during the 1840s which triggered some new laws in food standards and the RSPCA was formed in 1824.

A Victorian kitchen as shown in Mr Beeton's 1861 Book of Household Management.

The country house had food preparation areas such as the dairy, butchery, brewery and bakery, separate to the house. It had to have a well designed kitchen, a full range of specialist equipment and serving dishes, as well as staff trained in the arts of cooking, baking, carving, serving and a vast range of other roles. Robert Kerr published a book in 1864 entitled The Gentleman's House in which he provided great detail in the planning, building and running of the kitchen. He lists the rooms required (scullery, a dairy with its own scullery, a pantry, separate larders for the raw meat, bacon and fish, a smoking room, a salting room, the pastry room, a brewing house with cellars for beer and for wine and last, but not least, the bake house. It was common for larger houses to have at least five separate larders.

A small, simple Victorian kitchen where the lady of the house has been busy making biscuits. Pitstone Green Museum, Buckinghamshire.

The Victorians with a large household went to great lengths to keep the kitchen well away from the general entertaining and dining areas. Although this made it more difficult for staff to serve the food hot, it was thought exceptionally disgusting to have cooking aromas greeting the guests. Dining room warm cabinets became fashionable and a vast array of dish covers would serve to not only keep dishes warm, but essentially stop smells escaping as food was transferred to the dining area.

Kitchen fireplaces could easily be up to three metres wide and at least one metre deep – room enough to house the roasting range, and an oven, sometimes a boiler at the back. Roasting meat in front of the fire, gradually turning it, still remained one of the oldest and simplest forms of cooking. When stoves were developed they were warmly received by the kitchen staff and a 'show-off' item for the lady of the house.

All these specialist functions required specially trained staff and a large amount of equipment ranging from the large items such as ovens and ranges, tables, dressers, benches and boilers to the small items such as balances, chopping blocks, marble slabs, mills, mortars, specialised pans and a mass of other utensils.

Cooking utensils and methods are very interesting. Many are gaining new favour in modern television programmes presented by top chefs. There was much innovation in techniques such as the new steam ovens with their associated pans and equipment. Many utensils were just functional, while others imparted a special touch to the cuisine.

A selection of 'modern' stoves shown in Mrs Beeton's 1861 book which were transforming kitchen work.

KITCHEN UTENSILS.

A selection of essential utensils illustrated in Mrs Beeton's 1861 book.
1. Chafing dish pan; 2. Chafing dish stand and lamp; 3. Double boiler of chafing dish; 4. Jelly mould; 5. Meat slice; 6. Whisk;. 7. Chafing dish complete; 8. Colander; 9. Dutch oven; 10. Spice box. The chafing dish was a vessel with a heating element underneath and would keep food hot at the table.

Breakfast

Mary Hooper's 1873 *Handbook for the Breakfast Table* and A. Kenny Herbert's 1894 book *Fifty breakfasts* showed how important this meal was in Victorian times. A Victorian breakfast would contain boiled eggs, omelettes (special as fresh eggs were difficult to obtain), crispy bacon, home-made sausages (butchers were not trusted to make these – echoing today's sentiment that 'you never know what they put in them'!), smoked kippers, kedgeree, a range of cold meats, fancy bread (French or Vienna), oat cakes, scones, crumpets, griddled muffins and Sally Lunn buns amongst other baked items. All that baking meant the kitchen maids were up early kneading dough, setting the ovens and preparing the range of goodies on offer. The preferred breakfast drink was often cocoa, which was more popular than tea. Coffee was popular, but was heavily taxed and expensive.

Luncheon

This meal was often dubbed the 'inconsequent meal' as it was largely seen as a smaller replica of the evening meal (but with soup and fish never served). However, socially it fulfilled the role of being able to include those in society that were usually not invited to evening meals – for instance, pariahs such as single or elderly ladies! Traditionally it would be something easy to prepare and easy to eat such as sliced cold meats, meat galantine followed by rice pudding or suet pudding or roly-poly (plum or fig were popular) or stewed fruit with biscuits. It was also popular to have this meal as a picnic if the weather was suitable. Picnics seem to have become popular only from the early 19th century.

Five o'clock tea

The Duchess of Bedford is reputed to have 'invented' afternoon tea after explaining that she felt a sinking feeling of emptiness by the end of the afternoon. With a typical evening meal not to be served until between 7 and 8.30 pm, the canny Duchess started inviting her friends to her room for a light meal of sandwiches and cake – the afternoon tea was here. The Duchess was one of Queen Victoria's Ladies in Waiting and one of the cakes served at the tea was named after the Queen – the Victoria Sponge.

Almond pastries – ready for the 5 o'clock tea

This eating occasion began to be called 'At Homes' and women regarded them as socially very important events. However, men rather looked down on this predominantly female pastime thinking it unrestrained indulgence. Women on the other hand began to enjoy the link of light refreshment with a chance to meet friends and gossip.

Lardy cake – how it should look with a golden brown top and a gooey sugary base. This one is for the poorer table.

We may live without poetry, music and art.
We may live without conscience, and live without heart.
We may live without friends; we may live without books.
But civilised man cannot live without cooks.

He may live without books – what is knowledge but grieving?
He may live without hope – what is hope but deceiving?
He may live without love – what is passion but pining?
But where is the man that can live without dining?

Edward Robert Bulwer Lucile 1860

Dinner

There were lots of changes in etiquette during Victoria's reign, the result of which was to make dinner a more elegant affair, smaller and lighter dishes, but with numerous courses. There were so many courses it was thought polite by the end of the 19th century to provide a menu list of courses and wines so the guests could pace themselves.

A menu card from an 1899 dinner at Kings College.

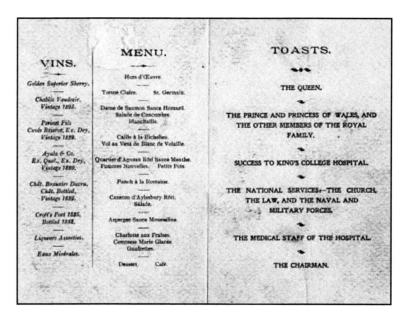

To ask for or to serve potatoes (a staple of the early Victorian era) would be thought of as vulgar by the end of Victoria's reign.

Menu
A very full menu might be along these lines:

Hors d'oeuvres: (in towns, not in the country)
Soup: to whet the appetite, a choice of a thick one and a consommé.
Fish course: turbot, salmon and sole were very popular
Meat course: a whole joint brought to the table served with vegetables and a salad
Sorbet: a pineapple was often incorporated into this as it was so expensive and exotic.
The roast course: roast rabbit, hare, turkey, pheasant or any selection of small birds (quail, snipe, woodcock, even larks).
Vegetable course: lightly cooked and without too much 'fuss' of elaborate sauces, etc.
Dessert: the household and cook ensured this was the crowning glory!
Savouries: such as chestnuts almonds, dessert sweetmeats
Ices: a wide variety was popular and needed an ice house to arrange
Fruit: if the house had pineapple in a hot-house then this would be paraded in, otherwise strawberries and cream, or other seasonal fruit.

A dish of dessert sweetmeats could consist of barley sugar, burnt almonds, butterscotch, caramels, fondant creams, marzipan treats, petits fours, toffee or Turkish Delight.

Supper
With the late dinner, suppers became much lighter, and no hot dishes served. Items such as cold meats, pates, salmon, toasted cheese, green leaf salad with watercress or mustard and cress (with the house dressing), Salmagundi salad, dried fruits, jellies or fruit creams were popular. But whatever was chosen would be light and aid digestion – which is why celery was often added to this meal.

Whatever the meal and whoever you were entertaining, the garnishing and serving were all important. Everything were lavishly decorated with cooks going to great lengths to prepare real cockscombs to add a decorative flair to poultry dishes, or crystallised violets, angelica, spun sugar and preserved fruits to adorn fancy moulded jellies were essential and would take many hours and planning in advance.

Invalid food
Mrs Beeton sums up the analytical approach beginning to be taken around illness. In her books she adds a section called Invalid cookery. Most recipes under this heading are liquid, although light meals of fish or chicken feature. Broths and soups feature in many forms, along with eggs in a variety of styles including 'egg nog' surprisingly. Lemonades and a medley of different teas were all proposed to have health benefitting effects.

Mrs Beeton, along with other Victorians, was convinced of the health properties of milk. This was seen as a perfect food source full of nature's goodness, but also powerful healing properties for healing a range of ailments including mental illness. Mrs Beeton's recipes included much more than rice pudding – tapioca, ground rice, sago, semolina, junket, milk jelly, blancmange, egg custard and ice creams all made full use of this adaptable nutritious product – milk.

Bread consumption changed enormously over this era. At the beginning Victorians were eating at least four times the amount of bread consumed in modern times. The price of bread was kept artificially high by the government. The price fell however when poor corn harvests were leading to famine and prices began rising even higher. In addition, technological inventions such as bread making machinery and advances in ovens ensured baking could go to large-scale manufacture, which meant it became much cheaper. Surprisingly, the result was to make bread unfashionable! It was suddenly seen as the poor person's food and hence aspiring households stopped purchasing it. Bakers, like any business under threat for survival, devised some new ideas to increase sales. Rolls and loaves were made into fancy shapes to look grand on any table. Highly refined (white) flour was introduced along with recipes for French rolls, dinner and bridge rolls which were enriched dough. Bread sales saw a little revival with these measures, but the biggest winner of them all was the opening of tea rooms. In 1864 the ABC Tearooms opened and in 1894 they were followed by the Lyons Tea Houses. For both, the clientele aimed at were women. Up to this point cafés and tearooms were only frequented by men. No respectable ladies would be seen out un-accompanied; hence meeting friends was not possible outside the home. The tearooms changed everything and quickly became used by females to meet friends for afternoon tea. This greatly increased the baker's profit – they could bake the bread on the premises and then sell the sandwiches at a much higher mark up.

Of course the menus and numerous books published during this era were aimed at the Middle to Upper class ladies. Books gave much advice on everything from the wording of invitations, table etiquette, hiring staff and butchery to table layout, place servings and recipes. However, there was great interest shown by poorer levels of society in what fine dining was like in the more affluent households. In this respect, any recipe seen to be enjoyed by the royal family was immediately adopted at all levels that could afford it – for instance Prince Albert Pudding, and see the later recipes for Victoria Sponge and Balmoral Shortbread. However, writers such as Mrs Beeton made space in their books on being frugal, not wasting food and offered a number of household tips that would save money. In her own words "Frugality and economy are home virtues". There were also recipes aimed at poorer households. One good example is her choice of recipe for caraway cake. Mrs Beeton's two versions are called 'Seed cake, Common' and 'Seed cake, Rich'. The former used bread dough with dripping, sugar, caraway seed and 1 egg (cost 9d). The latter was a true cake and used butter, 6 eggs, mace and nutmeg along with the other usual ingredients (cost 2s). The reader could thus assess what dishes suited their budget.

Dinner rolls, plaits and bridge bread rolls
This is a basic bread recipe, but the addition of margarine and milk make it an enriched dough.
450 g (1 lb) flour
60 g (2 oz) margarine
7 g (¼oz) salt
28 g (1 oz) fresh yeast
280 ml (10 fl oz) milk – makes 16 dinner rolls or 40 bridge rolls or 1 plait and 8 dinner rolls

Scald the milk and allow to cool. Rub the fat into the flour. Put salt into half the milk which is at room temperature/just warm; cream the fresh yeast into the other half. Strain into two separate wells in the flour. Mix with the hand, then turn out onto a board and knead for 7 to 10 minutes.
Leave aside in a covered bowl in a warm place for about 30 minutes. Turn out onto floured board and 'knock back', kneading it well and then leaving again for 20 minutes in the warm.
Divide the dough according to whether you are making plaits, dinner or bridge rolls. Shape and leave on a warm, greased and floured baking tin for about 15 minutes.
Glaze with an egg-milk wash and cook in a hot oven at 240 C (475 F) for 10 minutes (rolls) or 20 minutes (the plait). When done the bottom will sound hollow when tapped.

The Victorian 5 O'Clock tea
Sandwiches (very finely cut): ham, cucumber, tongue, bone marrow with nasturtium leaves
Scones, butter, jam and cream
Biscuits: Macaroons, Balmoral shortbread
Caraway seed cake and Victoria Sandwich cake

A traditional 'At Home' tea would involve drinking tea, coffee, wine, sherry, a claret cup or a champagne cup accompanied by wafer thin sandwiches, fancy biscuits, cakes, fruit and ice creams. Popular cakes were Madeira, Caraway seed cake, fruit cake and a Victoria sponge. The Victoria sponge was an unusual addition to tea – as until the Queen expressed a liking for it, sponge cakes were only deemed fit for the nursery tea and children. Early Victorian teas for adults had sandwiches of only ham, beef or tongue. Cucumber is now a traditional sandwich for a tea but it was not used until later Victorian times as it was at first believed to be poisonous and bad for the constitution.

"Beautiful soup! Who cares for fish, game, or any other dish? Who would not give all else for two pennyworth only of beautiful soup?" **Lewis Carroll.**

Jerusalem artichoke soup
2 lb artichokes, washed & cut into small pieces or slices (Serves 6)
½ turnip, cut into small pieces
½ onion, chopped
4 sticks celery, sliced thinly
1½ oz butter
2 slices back bacon, fat trimmed off, small pieces
2½ pints vegetable or chicken stock and ½ pint milk
1 tablespoon cream
Salt & pepper

Put the butter, bacon, celery, turnip and onion into a large pan. Sweat for 15 minutes stirring regularly to prevent browning. Add artichokes and only ½ pint of the stock and simmer until very soft and breaking down. Add salt & pepper and pass through a sieve (you can cheat by using a blender here). Return to pan, add remaining stock, simmer for a further 5 minutes. Add milk and cream, heat through but do not allow to the boil. Serve with croutons.

Mock Turtle Soup

This is a popular recipe from a very popular cookbook Dr Kitchener's The Cook's Oracle, which was republished many times to appear in 1861 as the Shilling Kitchener.

225 g (8oz) stewing beef, diced
2 back bacon rashers
1 carrot, chopped
Sprigs (1 each of) of mixed herbs: lemon thyme, winter savoury, basil (if dried, tie in muslin)
Good handful fresh parsley
2 shallots, chopped
1 whole onion with 4 cloves inserted
15 allspice berries and 15 black peppercorns
2 tablespoons flour
120 ml (4 fl oz) sherry
Juice of ½ lemon
2 teaspoons mushroom ketchup
Good grate of nutmeg
Salt & pepper
150 ml (5fl oz) water, followed by 1.8 litres (3 pints) water

Place beef, bacon, carrot, shallots and onion with herbs, spices and water into a large pan. Bring to the boil and simmer for 15 minutes. Then add the 1.8 litres (3 pints) of water, bring back to the boil and simmer on a very low heat for 2 hours.
Mix a little of the soup with the flour in a small bowl to make a paste, returning it to the pan stirring continuously, to thicken the soup and then cook for a further 30 minutes.
Strain the soup through a fine sieve and return to a clean pan (beef can be picked out and returned to the soup). Add sherry, mushroom ketchup, lemon juice and nutmeg with the seasoning. Gently reheat and serve.

Fricasseed soles

Mrs Beeton's recipe

2 middling-sized soles, and 1 small one (Serves 4)
½ teaspoon chopped lemon-peel
1 teaspoonful chopped parsley
a little grated bread
salt, pepper, and nutmeg to taste
1 egg
2oz butter
½ pint of good gravy
2 tablespoons of port wine
Cayenne and lemon-juice to taste

Fry the soles to brown and drain them well from the fat. Take all the flesh from the small
sole, chop it fine, and mix with it the lemon-peel, parsley, bread and seasoning; work altogether, with the yolk of an egg and the butter; make this into small balls, and fry them. Thicken the gravy with a dessertspoon of flour, add the port wine, cayenne, and lemon juice; lay in the 2 soles and balls; let them simmer gently for 6 minutes; serve hot, and garnish with cut lemon. Time: 10 minutes to fry the soles.

Stewed lettuce

The Romans had their cooked lettuce dish, and here is a Victorian version to accompany meat.
The author found both recipes a disgusting flavour and texture, although this recipe was the better. Both in Roman and Victorian times this dish was prepared more for health reasons than enjoyment.

1 whole lettuce, remove outer leaves & stalks, wash
½oz butter
Flour
Small cup of stock or consommé
Salt & pepper to taste
Squeeze of lemon juice

Bring some salted water to the boil and add the lettuce leaves. Simmer for c. 20 minutes and then drain and pat with kitchen towelling to remove excess water. Chop and place in fresh saucepan with butter and seasoning. Sprinkle in a little flour and stirring all the time gradually add the stock/consommé. Boil rapidly to allow liquid to evaporate and reduce to moist mixture. Add splash of lemon juice and serve.

Bordyke Veal Cake

A recipe from Eliza Acton that she says is also 'excellent cold'. A tasty version of the meat loaf. Serves 10

675 g (1½ lb) stewing veal
225 g (8oz) back bacon
Grated rind of 2 lemons
½ teaspoon mace
¼ teaspoon cayenne

Mince the veal and bacon with the coarse setting, mix in lemon rind and spices. Press the mixture into a loaf tin which is lined with greaseproof.
Cook in an oven set to 180°C (Gas mark 4) for 45 minutes. Remove immediately from the tin so that any fat may drain from it. Serve with salad and boiled potatoes.

Breast of lamb and green peas
1 breast of lamb (Serves 3)
5 slices of bacon
140 ml (¼ pint) of stock
1 lemon
1 onion
1 bunch of savoury herbs
3 large cups of green peas

Remove the skin from a breast of lamb, put it into a saucepan of boiling water, and let it simmer for 5 minutes. Take it out and lay it in cold water. Line the bottom of a stewing pan with three thin slices of bacon; lay the lamb on these. Peel the lemon, cut it into slices, and put these on the meat, to keep it white and make it tender. Cover with 2 more slices of bacon; add the stock, onion and herbs, and simmer very gently until tender. Have ready some green peas, put these on a dish, and place the lamb on the top of these. The appearance of this dish may be much improved by glazing the lamb, and spinach may be substituted for the peas when variety is desired.
Time: 1½hours. (quoted as: "average cost, 10d. per lb. Seasonable - grass lamb, from Easter to Michaelmas").

Quoorma curry

Mrs Beeton's recipe for this Indian dish influenced by the British colonisation of India. Mrs Beeton's book All about cookery lists: American, Canadian, Australian and Indian dishes along with French, German, Austrian, Italian and Passover dishes under her heading of 'Colonial and Foreign Cookery'.

 500 g (1 lb) lean mutton
60 g (2oz) butter
90 g (3 oz) shallots, finely chopped
1 clove of garlic, very finely chopped
1 dessertspoon finely grated green ginger

1 dessertspoon rice flour
1 teaspoon ground coriander seed
1 teaspoon ground black pepper
½ teaspoon ground cardamoms
½ teaspoon ground cloves
1 teaspoon ground turmeric
1 'saltspoon' of sugar
560 ml (1 pint) mutton stock and 280 ml (½ pint) milk
60 g (2oz) ground almonds
Juice of 1 lemon
Salt

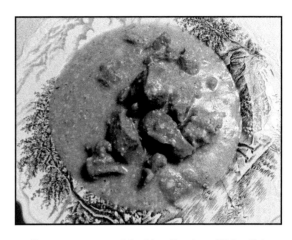

Quoorma curry à la Mrs Beeton. This dish tastes very nice, but without chilli and with lemon juice added, it had a rather French style about it. It was clearly influenced by colonial India, but the French fashion was still a stronger influence at this time.

Cut the meat into small squares; sprinkle the ginger and salt to season and leave for about an hour. Melt the butter in a stew pan, fry the shallots and garlic until lightly browned, then add the rice flour, coriander, pepper, cardamoms and cloves and cook gently for 10 minutes. Add the stock, bring to the boil and simmer gently for 15 minutes, then pour over the meat and let it stand, covered, for 30 minutes. Turn it into a stewpan, bring to the boil and then simmer very slowly for 30 minutes or until the meat is perfectly tender. In the meantime soak the pounded amonds in the milk and when the meat is tender strain the milk 2 or 3 times through fine muslin, pressing the almonds well each time, then add it to the contents of the stewpan. Mix the turmeric with a little stock or water and stir it in, add the sugar and salt to taste. Continue to cook slowly on a very low heat for another 20 minutes. Add the lemon juice just before serving.
Mrs Beeton says "Average cost 1s 7d to 1s 9d; sufficient for 4 persons".

Salmagundi
This popular salad can contain all sorts of salad vegetables, as long as it is layered attractively and colourful contrasts throughout. The Georgians had their own version of this meal but served as individual tiny tasters.

Hard boiled eggs, shelled and sliced
Chicken, cooked and cut into small, neat slices
Ham, cut off the bone or rolled into 'tubes'
Tongue, sliced neatly
Pickled red cabbage; Beetroot
Anchovies
Parsley to decorate

Place a tiny bowl or teacup in the centre of a dish or plate. Start with layering the eggs across the plate to the centre. Then continue the layers with each of the ingredients – each successive layer gets less wide so the bottom layers remain visible in ever decreasing circles. End with a decorative array of anchovies and parsley – all very neatly placed.

Salsifis à la Crème
A recipe from Charles Francatelli who became the Royal chef from about 1840.

900 g (2lb) salsify, peeled and cut into 3 cm (1 inch) pieces
10 g (¼ oz) butter
Juice of 1 lemon
4 tablespoons Béchamel sauce
Salt & pepper

Prepare and cut the salsify, but leave covered in the cooking pan by water with the lemon juice to stop it discolouring. It will then be ready to cook when the dish it is to accompany is ready. When it is 12 minutes before required bring to the boil and simmer until cooked (c. 10 minutes), beware of it turning mushy. Drain and add the butter, béchamel sauce and season. Taste to check if further lemon juice or seasoning is required, and serve.

Vegetable Marrows in white sauce
Another Mrs Beeton special

4 or 5 moderate-sized marrows (Serves 5 to 6)
300 ml (½ pint) of white sauce

Pare the marrows; cut them in halves, and shape each half at the top in a point, leaving the bottom end flat for it to stand upright in the dish. Boil the marrows in salted water until tender Take them up very carefully, and arrange them on a hot dish. Have ready 1/2 pint of white sauce; pour this over the marrows, and serve. Time: From 15 to 20 minutes to boil the marrows. (Quoted as: "average cost, in full season, 1s. per dozen. Seasonable in July, August, and September".)

Marrow toast
A popular supper dish

1 marrow bone, broken by your butcher
Slices of (thin) toast, only lightly toasted
Salt & pepper to season
Parsley, finely chopped

Take out the marrow and place the pieces in a pan with a little salted water. Bring to the boil, hold the boil for one minute, then strain through a fine sieve. Place the marrow on the toast and pop under a very low grill (in front of the fire for the Victorians) until cooked (3 minutes?). Season and serve immediately.

Croquettes de Macaroni au Fromage de Stilton
A recipe from Alexis Soyer and the Reform Club, a renowned French chef. This tasty supper dish can be made in advance and reheated.

150 g (5 oz) small macaroni
20 g (¾ oz) butter
20 g (¾ oz) flour
450 ml (15 fl oz) full fat milk
225 g (15 fl oz Stilton (blue for stronger flavour, white for milder), grated
Salt & pepper, and cayenne
Good grate of nutmeg
3 egg yolks
2 whole beaten eggs
3 good handfuls brown breadcrumbs
Oil for frying

Cook the macaroni until al dente, drain it and return to the pan to keep warm. Melt butter in another pan add the flour to make a roux, adding milk gradually to make a sauce.
Add the macaroni, cheese and seasonings, followed by the egg yolks, cook so as to set the yolks. Remove the pan from the heat, put to one side until totally cold.
Use a small dessert spoon to spoon and shape the mixture into ovals. Each croquette should be coated with beaten egg and rolled in a generous coating of breadcrumbs.
Heat the oil in a pan frying the croquettes for about 2 to 3 minutes until brown, crisp but not burnt. Present them piled into a pyramid on a napkin and serve hot.

Hot eel pie

Street food for the lower classes. In the day you would need to take care with this one as poor vendors might have used already dead large eels. This one is based on a Kettner recipe.

900 g (2 lb) small eels, cut into sections
4 shallots, chopped finely
3 bouquet garni
Salt & pepper, good grate of nutmeg
300 ml (10 fl oz) sherry
50 g (2 oz) butter
50 g (2 oz) flour (wholemeal)
Juice of 1 lemon
4 hard boiled eggs, sliced
675g (1½ lb) puff pastry (Victorians would make this, I recommend buying it!)

Put eel, shallots, and all seasoning into a pan with sherry and enough water to cover. Simmer for c. 2 minutes. Take out the eel and arrange in a pie dish with the hard boiled eggs.
Melt butter in a pan, add the flour to make a roux. Remove pan from the heat and then slowly add 900 ml (1½ pints) of the cooking liquid to the roux, stirring continuously. Return pan to the heat, bring to the boil slowly, stirring until it thickens.. Season to taste, add lemon juice, pour over the eels in the dish. Cover with a pastry lid and bake for about 25 minutes at 190°C (375 F or gas mark 5) when it will be golden brown. Can be eaten hot or cold.

Gooseberry Fool

Mrs Beeton's recipe with her comments and quantities left in place.
Green gooseberries; to every pint of pulp add 1pint of milk, or 1/2 pint of cream and 1/2 pint of milk; and sugar to taste.

Cut the tops and tails off the gooseberries; put them into a jar, with 2 tablespoons of water and a little good moist sugar; set this jar in a saucepan of boiling water, and let it boil until the fruit is soft enough to mash. When done enough, beat it to a pulp, work this pulp through a colander, and stir to every pint the above proportion of milk, or equal quantities of milk and cream.
Ascertain if the mixture is sweet enough, and put in plenty of sugar, or it will not be eatable; and in mixing the milk and gooseberries, add the former very gradually to these: serve in a glass dish, or in small glasses.
This, although a very old-fashioned and homely dish, is, when well made, very delicious, and, if properly sweetened, a very suitable preparation for children.
Time: From 3/4 to 1 hour. Average cost, 6d. per pint, with milk.
Sufficient: A pint of milk and a pint of gooseberry pulp for 5 or 6 children.

A selection of desserts from Mrs Beeton's book showing how to display them with elegance and skill in the assembly and decoration.

1. Pancakes; 2. Rice and apple cake; 3. Éclairs; 4. Assorted pastry; 5. Rice pudding; 6. Stewed fruits;
7. Pyramid cream; 8. Croquettes of rice; 10. Gâteau St. Honoré;
11. Simnel cake.

Strawberry ice cream

A lovely traditional recipe from Mrs Beeton's cookbook with her comments and quantities included.

1 lb strawberries
½ pint cream
¼ pint milk
3 yolks of eggs
10 oz castor sugar
1 teaspoon lemon juice
Carmine

Bring the milk and cream to near boiling point, add the beaten egg yolks, stir by the side of the fire until they thicken, then put in the sugar, and when dissolved strain and let the preparation cool. Pass the strawberries through a fine sieve, mix with the custard, add the lemon juice and carmine gradually until a deep pink colour is obtained. Then freeze. Time: about 1 hour. Average cost 2s. to 2s. 3d. Sufficient for 7 to 8 persons.

Lemon cup cakes

Mrs Beeton's recipe was for a medium size cake, here made into cup cakes with lemon icing in honour of the Lyons Corner Houses. Lemon cup cakes were one of the popular cakes served at Lyons Corner Houses all over Britain. From 1894 until 1977 the 'Nippy Waitress' was well-known for literally being 'nippy' and giving quick and efficient service of tea and cake to its customers.

8 eggs
1 tablespoon orange flower water
230 g (8 oz) castor sugar
1 lemon
460 g (1 lb) flour

Break the eggs into a basin and add the sugar and beat to a stiff batter with a wire egg-whisk (cheat and use electric if you like!). Add the orange flower water, the juice and rind of 1 lemon and continue beating for 10 minutes, then take out the whisk, clean it off and add the flour (sifted), mix this with a spoon. Butter a cake mould with melted butter, dust it with a little flour and sugar mixed, turn in the mixture (I used paper cases in a cup cake tin). Bake in a moderate oven 180 C (375 F) for about 20 minutes or until done (A large cake would be c. 1½ hours and may need covering to prevent over-browning. The lemon icing was simply icing sugar and more lemon juice allowed to set in the cases before serving. Mrs Beeton says they"Cost 1s 4d"

Scotch Shortbread

Mrs Beeton's recipe – enough for 6 rounds or squares which she calls 'cakes'.
920 g (2 lb) flour and 115 g (4oz) cornflour or ground rice
460 g (1 lb) butter
115 g (4 oz) castor sugar
28 g (1 oz) sweet almonds, blanched and cut into small pieces
A few strips of candied orange peel

Beat the butter to a cream, gradually dredge in the flour, and add the sugar and sweet almonds. Work the paste until it is quite smooth, and divide it into 6 pieces. Put each cake on a separatepiece of paper, roll the paste out square to the thickness of about 1 inch (2.5 cm) and pinch around the edges. Prick it well with a skewer, and ornament with 1 or 2 strips of candied orange peel. Put the cakes into a moderate oven 180 C (375 F) and bake for 25 to 30 minutes. Mrs Beeton says "the cost is 2 s".

Balmoral shortbread

To make this royal shortbread (from the palace recipes) make as above from flour, butter and castor sugar only. Make shortbread into rectangular fingers and prick with a fork. The fork pattern was always the same – three rows of three dots (in a domino pattern). It is reputed that Queen Victoria ate this shortbread every day.

Victoria Sandwich

A variation of the sponge named for the Queen and became
exceptionally popular as it still is today.
225 g (8 oz) butter
225 g (8 oz) castor sugar
225 g (8 oz) flour
4 eggs
Grated rind of 1 lemon and a pinch of salt
Jam for the filling (recipes below)
Icing sugar to decorate

Place butter and sugar in a bowl and beat with a wooden spoon
until pale and soft. Beat in the eggs one at a time (slowly or they will curdle). Fold in the sieved flour and salt with a metal spoon (figure of 8 motion) and add the lemon rind. Pour the mixture into a large sponge tin (to split when cold) or two tins and bake for 20 minutes (for the latter) at 180 C (350 F).
When cool fill with your favourite jam, dust with icing sugar and serve immediately. Delicious. This is photographed in the 5-O'clock tea.

Tipsy cake

A really delicious cake from Mrs Beeton which is very simple to make.
1 stale/dry sponge cake (e.g. Victoria sponge type)
6 tablespoons brandy
300 ml (10 fl oz) medium sherry
50 g (2 oz) flaked almonds, lightly toasted in oven
600 ml (1 pint) creamy custard or enough cream to serve with a slice

Arrange the whole cake on the serving plate/stand. Prick all over with a skewer. Mix the brandy with the sherry and pour all over the cake so it soaks it all up and goes soggy. (If the cake is very dry, then add some more.) Arrange the almonds all over the cake by sticking them into the cake and arranging as a pattern (sticking out like rays). Serve with the custard or whipped cream.

Treacle Pudding
A suet pud tradition thanks to the Stuarts and still a favourite! This recipe from Mrs Black's 1869 *Household Cookery*.

4 oz currants (Serves up to 6)
4 oz suet
1 cup breadcrumbs
I cup self-raising flour
1 tablespoon sugar
1 egg
8 oz treacle
1 teaspoon ginger
½teaspoon bicarbonate of soda
½ teaspoon cream of tartar
½ teaspoon salt
1 cup of water

Put flour, breadcrumbs, currants, sugar, suet, carbonate of soda and cream of tartar , ginger and salt into a bowl and mix well before adding the treacle and continue the mixing. Add the egg and water. Mix again. The mixture should be very moist, but not sloppy. Prepare a basin by coating it with butter inside and then spoon in the mixture. Cover top with buttered paper. Place into pan with half an inch of boiling water, and steam for 2½ hours. Serve with custard or cream. Very sweet and the ginger gives a little something special.

Christmas Plum Pudding
This recipe comes from Charles E. Francatelli's book *A plain cookery book for the working classes* 1861.
1½ lb plain flour   (Serves 8)
½ lb breadcrumbs
1 lb suet
12 oz currants; 12 oz raisins
12 oz apples, peeled & finely chopped
12 oz sugar
½ oz allspice
1½ pints milk or beer
4 eggs
Pinch salt

Mix the flour, suet and all fruit in a large pan. Add sugar, allspice and salt with half of the milk, mix. Then add the eggs and remaining milk. Mix vigorously – this would be with the hand of course! Wrap your pudding in a well greased cloth. Bring water to boil before placing the pudding in the pan and boiling for 4 hours.

Claret cup
Claret, 1 bottle
Soda water 1 medium bottle
2 glasses dry sherry
A good grating of nutmeg
8 cloves
2 tablespoons sugar
Juice and rind of 1/3 lemon
Sprig of borage if available, or 6 small leaves mint

Into a quart vessel put in all the ingredients but only a small amount of the claret, stir and leave for 20 minutes. Remove cloves and lemon peel with a spoon. Add soda and remainder of the claret, serve.

Champagne cup

1 bottle of champagne
1 liqueur glass of brandy
2 bottles of seltzer or soda water
½ teaspoon Maraschino
A few fine strips of lemon peel

Mrs Beeton says: When the time permits it is much better to ice the liquor which forms the basis of a 'cooling cup' than to reduce the temperature by adding ice. Place the champagne and selzer in a deep vessel, surround them with ice. Cover them with a wet woollen cloth, and let them remain for 1 hour. When ready to serve put the strips of lemon into a large glass jug, add the Maraschino and brandy, pour in the soda water and serve at once. If liked a teaspoon of sugar may be added, but it should be stirred in gradually, otherwise the wine may overflow.

Homemade Jam

There is nothing tastier than homemade jam. The recipes have hardly changed over the years. When this jam goes into your cakes, your cakes enter a different league!

Strawberry Jam or Raspberry Jam

Mrs Beeton says: To each 1lb (460 g) of fruit allow 12 to 16 oz (350 to 460 g) of preserving sugar.
For the raspberry the quantity is 1:1 plus a ¼ pint (140 ml) redcurrant juice.
Remove the stalk from the fruit, place in a preserving pan, sprinkle on the sugar, place on the heat and bring very gradually to boiling point, stirring all the time. Skim well and boil gently until the setting point is reached (stirring occasionally). Pour into warmed pots with a greaseproof disc and lid. Label and store in a cool, dry place.

Plum jam

The proportions of fruit to sugar is the same as above and depends on your preferred sweetness and the acidity of the chosen plums. The plums need dividing and the stone removed. The sugar is placed over the fruit but this time left overnight. Cooking is as above.

The Aylesbury prune (right) - a name given to a heritage variety of plum, full flavoured and very much in demand due to the quality of the fruit. The name was given due to the large orchards growing near Aylesbury and in fact in large parts of the whole county of Buckinghamshire. These were harvested from the author's tree.

Plum ginger and cinnamon jam

This is a delicious variation of the plum jam that I make every year. It is worth making a lot of this one – hence the larger quantities:
3 lb plums, de-stoned
3 lb preserving sugar
1 teaspoon cinnamon; 1 teaspoon ginger (powdered form)
Knob of butter
¼ pint water

Bring plums to boil in the water, about 20 to 30 minutes until soft. Add sugar stirring continuously until dissolved and stir in the spices. When setting point is reached stir in the butter. Pour into pots as above.

15.

Edwardian eating – upstairs and downstairs

Fiddly cooking for the upper class, but some basic classics for those 'downstairs'.

This was a period of excesses with lots of courses, servants to cook and serve them, and very strict etiquette. Similar to the Victorian style of cooking dishes contained a lot of butter, eggs and cream, but also fresh fruit when in season, and seafood such as lobster, shrimps and oysters along with popular whiting and sole. Of course, this was if you could afford it. From 1886 it was noted that more than 25% of adult males earned less than 20 shillings per week and this was still the same in 1914. The largest part of this income (60%) went on food. For this reason expensive items such as meat and dairy foods were eaten in small quantities – the staples being bread and potatoes. The man, being the breadwinner, would take the lion's share of the food, which meant meals for the rest of the family were not always on a regular basis.

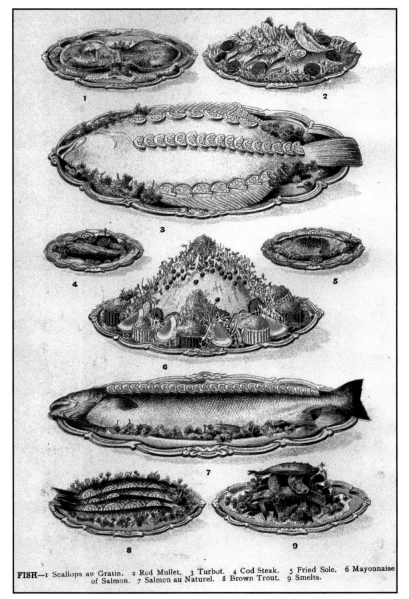

FISH—1 Scallops au Gratin. 2 Red Mullet. 3 Turbot. 4 Cod Steak. 5 Fried Sole. 6 Mayonnaise of Salmon. 7 Salmon au Naturel. 8 Brown Trout. 9 Smelts.

*Fish. A page from Mrs Beaton's 1909 reprint of her recipe book **All about cookery.** This book went through several reprints as it remained as popular as ever during Edwardian times.*

Meat of all kinds (including unusual parts of the animal never eaten today such as brains) was cooked in many ways. These dishes were accompanied by a wealth of fresh vegetables and herbs. Spices such as ginger, nutmeg, cinnamon and cloves continued to be important – we seem to have always loved our spices. Keen to imitate the upper classes the middle classes strived to serve multiple courses, which of course required staff to assist in the preparation, cooking and serving. This became especially true as dishes became more complex. Sauces especially became very skilful, rich and ever more delicious. Cider was a popular drink for this period and farm workers were often paid in cider!

Joints. A page from Mrs Beaton's 1909 reprint of her recipe book All about cookery. Even a joint must be decorated attractively to serve at the table and make the spectacle of the carving.

JOINTS—1 Sirloin of Beef. 2 Boiled Beef. 3 Leg of Mutton. 4 Roast Ribs of Beef.

By the very end of the Edwardian period attitudes towards menus and cooking began to get a little more relaxed. This was a period of massive changes for workers such as the house servants. Many servants had begun to drift into factory work as it was better paid. As workers were awarded a half day off in the factories as well, it became clear that households would need to compete in order to retain staff. An increase in wages and a half day off meant that the lady of the house had to start assisting the kitchen staff. However, this was made slightly easier by new technology - gas cookers made a big entrance – it is estimated that very quickly up to 10% of households had this new piece of equipment. Although they would not pass modern safety regulations by any means, they did make cooking cleaner and easier.

Vegetables. A page from Mrs Beaton's 1909 reprint of her recipe book All about cookery

VEGETABLES—1 Braized Celery. 2 Leeks. 3 Boiled Seakale. 4 Brussels Sprouts. 5 Baked Potatoes. 6 Parsnips. 7 Boiled Potatoes. 8 Artichokes. 9 Cabbage. 10 Braized Onions.

New technology also made it possible to tin food to preserve it. Tinned food was very popular and store cupboards would be filled with it in the middle and upper class households. Some tinned items were held in high esteem. For instance many types were stocked with pride at Fortnum and Mason and would be served at meals to impress your dinner party guests!

However, changes were afoot and vegetarianism became more common with the Food Reform Movement proposing a healthy diet of less meat, more vegetables, fruit, wholemeal bread, nuts and lentils. The suffragette movement supported the following of a vegetarian diet.

As with the Victorians, an Edwardian picnic was a very popular family event. Laid out with full cloths, napkins and cutlery, glasses and a wonderful array of pate, chicken, raised pies, salad and cakes baked to be easily transportable without breaking and to be absolutely delicious.

Utensils. A page from Mrs Beaton's 1909 reprint of her recipe book All about cookery showing more modern equipment to her earlier book.
1. Household weighing machine; 2. Oval boiling pot; 3. Turbot kettle; 4. Copper preserving pan; 5. Fish kettle; 6. Bain marie pans; 7. Iron stockpot with tap; 8. Saucepan and steamer; 9. Steak tongs; 10. Fish slice.

An Edwardian picnic with whole (tinned) sardines in the fish dish, pate and a soft cheese with bread – all carried out in the Fortnam and Mason's hamper basket.

The picnic would not be complete without the ever popular pork raised pie.

Chicken and ham raised pie

This could also be made with veal and ham, beef or pork

225 g (8 oz) hot water crust pastry
350 g (12 oz) chicken
115 g (4 oz) ham or bacon
A little grated lemon rind
½ teaspoon chopped parsley (use sage for pork pie; garlic, parsley and thyme for beef)
½ teaspoon salt
Good sprinkle of pepper
1 hard boiled egg
2 tablespoons stock
Egg wash
90 ml (3 fl oz) jellied stock (using a good ½ teaspoon gelatine)

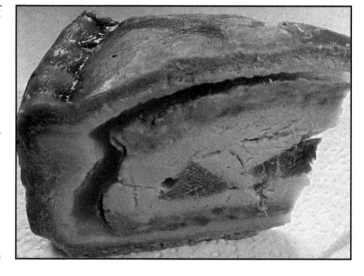

Make the pastry leaving a quarter to one-third for the lid, leaving it in a warm place.
Line a suitable size rectangular or circular greased tin (e.g. 15 cm or 6 inch diameter) with the pastry and draw it up the sides to line the tin to the top.

Cut the meat into small dice or mince it. Mix with the other ingredients for the filling. Press it into the pastry case, placing the hard-boiled egg into the centre of the pie. If using differently coloured meat then use your skill and imagination to make an attractive pattern to emerge once cut.

Roll out the lid slightly larger than the top of the pie to allow for sealing the edge. Wet the edges of the pastry, put on the lid, seal the edges, cut the edge with scissors and decorate the edge.
Make a hole in the centre of the lid, brush with egg wash and decorate with pastry leaves or other design from the pastry trimmings. Brush the decoration with egg wash.

Bake for 10 to 20 minutes at 200 °C until beginning to brown, then reduce the heat, cover the top with paper and allow to cook through gently at about 170-180 °C until the meat is completely cooked (about 2½ hours). Cool, and when totally cold, pour in the jellied stock which should be on the point of setting when added.

Elderflower syrup

1.7 litres (3 pints) boiling water
1.7 kg (3½ pounds) granulated sugar
3 lemons sliced
20 heads of elderflower
55 g (2 oz) tartaric acid/citric acid

Boil water and pour over sugar in a large bowl, add the rest of the ingredients and steep overnight. Strain and bottle into sterilised jars.

Use more lemons for a nice lemony tang, and if liked, slip in a few more elderflower heads. Tartaric acid is the item in the recipes, but this can be hard to come by, so citric acid can be used instead.

Elderflower syrup – delicate and refreshing. Photo: Julia Haworth.

Shrewsbury cake

1 lb castor sugar
1 lb butter
1½ lb flour
½ gill milk (or cream)
1 egg
Caraway seeds (optional)

Rub sugar, butter and flour together. Mix into a paste with the milk and egg. Rest for 30 minutes. Roll out and cut into small, round cakes. Bake in a moderate oven. Add caraway seeds if liked.

Eggs and artichokes

Boil artichokes and remove leaves and the choke. Make them hot in butter, sprinkle with salt and pepper and a few drops of lemon juice. Poach some eggs, trim them neatly and put an egg on each artichoke and place on a round of fried bread. Arrange on a hot dish and pour fresh tomato sauce over all.

Kidneys and tomatoes

Cut 3 kidneys in half, remove the skin and core. Cut 6 thick slices of raw tomato. Have ready some hot butter mixed with pepper, salt and chopped parsley. Fry 6 croutons of bread a nice golden colour and keep them hot. Boil or fry the kidneys and slices of tomato, place a slice of tomato on each crouton and then one kidney half. Pour the hot butter mixture over this and serve immediately.

Lobster Cream

Put ½ pint of cream into a bowl, add a good amount of salt, pepper, and cayenne, and whip until stiff. Add lobster pieces (about half a lobster worth) and spoon into dishes. Decorate with herbs and tiny shake of pepper or other attractive garnish.

Cheese straws

Mix ¼ lb flour, 3 oz grated cheese, salt and cayenne with the yolk of an egg and form into a firm paste. Roll out thinly into a rectangle. Cut into strips about the thickness of a little finger. Twist the strips as you lay them onto a floured baking tray. Bake in a moderate oven until crisp.

Cheese straws – crisp and a delight, go easy on the cayenne unless you want the straws to pack a little punch.

Faggots

A dish for those 'downstairs'

1½lb pig's liver

½lb fat pork

Teaspoon each of finely chopped herbs such as parsley, thyme, sage

1 onion, finely chopped

2 eggs

½ pint breadcrumbs

Lots of seasoning, especially pepper (1 teaspoon)

A little nutmeg

Pigs caul, or natural membrane to form faggots

Finely mince all meat, add seasoning and remaining ingredients – reserving the breadcrumbs and egg to one side for the moment. Place in a bowl, cover and place bowl in a pan with simmering water for 1 hour. When cool enough to handle, add breadcrumbs and egg, form into little balls and wrap around with the caul to hold them together, place in a baking dish. Bake until brown and cooked, about 30 minutes. Serve with gravy, potatoes and vegetables in season.

Faggots – steaming hot, inexpensive, tasty, wholesome and filling.

The Marlborough soufflé

Place ¼ pint double cream, 1 tablespoon flour, 2 oz castor sugar and 2 tablespoons desiccated coconut into a bowl and mix. Pour in a further ¼ pint boiling cream. Transfer the whole mixture to the pan and boil with care. Put to one side until cool. Add a small jar of shred-free orange (or lemon) marmalade. Separate 3 eggs and whip yolks and whites separately, so as to trap air in the white, which should be soft peak stage. Add both to the main mixture. Pour into tiny ramekin dishes and bake in moderate oven for 10 minutes until risen and set. Shake over with a fine dust of icing sugar and serve immediately.

Boston Apple Pudding

Sweet Lark was a popular Edwardian apple and this would need less sugar then any cooking apple, so sweeten to taste.

18 apples, peeled, cored and cut into small slices

4 oz butter

2 cloves and ½ nutmeg

Lemon peel, and rind and juice of 1 lemon

Cinnamon

Sugar to taste

Puff pastry

4 egg yolks, 1 white

Put apples in a pan with a little water, the cloves, cinnamon and lemon peel. Simmer until soft, sweeten to taste. Pass the apple mixture through a sieve. Add the egg yolks and white and the grated lemon rind and juice with the butter and nutmeg. Mix well together. Line a dish with the pastry, put the mixture in this and bake for 30 minutes.

Scones

230 g (8 oz) flour
Pinch of salt
60 g (2 oz) butter
1 tablespoon castor sugar
1 teaspoon cream of tartar*
½ teaspoon bicarbonate of soda*
45 g (1½) oz castor sugar
120 ml (4 fl oz) milk
(*or replace these two with 2 teaspoons of baking powder)

Sift together the flour, salt and raising agent*. Cut and rub in the butter. Add the sugar. Mix lightly with the milk to give a soft dough. Turn onto a floured board and roll to about half an inch thick and cut into round shapes with 2 inch cutters. Place on greased baking sheet, brush with milk and bake in a hot oven for 7 to 10 minutes. When cool serve with home-made jam and clotted cream.

A cream tea for Edwardians could be streamlined to scones, jam and cream for those with less cash to spare, but who want the treat of an outing to a tearoom. Here the choice is blackcurrant or strawberry jam.

16.

War time recipes from WWII

 Waste not, want not; make do with what you can find and substitute; learn new techniques to make nutritious meals on rations, and dig for Victory!

Food is one of the casualties of war. As imports of food become reduced ingredients need to be sourced elsewhere, used frugally, or substitutes made if possible. The Ministry of Food gave out lots of advice and many recipes during and after the war years. Reading any of the contemporary literature it soon becomes clear that the housewife was expected to fight on the kitchen front!

Some home grown and storable items were usually available, but could be in short supply and hence they were rationed. Rationing of many essential foods continued from 1940 to 1954. However, even non-rationed items took stealth and ingenuity to source – as and when available – as they were readily snapped up. A black market soon developed to supply selected items for a price. Other items could be grown if the household had a garden or allotment, leading to the call to 'Dig for Victory!' Many of the allotments people use today had their opening during the war years.

A table laid for tea with ration documents in view. Pitstone Farm Museum.

"Yes we have no bananas." A line from a song making fun of the common response from greengrocers to requests from housewives eager to purchase this much-loved item, but which were no longer available!

Imported foods soon became in short supply as merchant ships were unable to get through treacherous oceans and meet demand. Potatoes were generally in good supply and were used for many roles from padding out dishes to substituting for flour. Carrots were generally abundant too and carrot cake became popular due to the rationing of sugar. Cod was in reasonable supply and often replaced scarcer meat for the main meals. The drawback was that the cod was often supplied as salt-cod which requires 48 hours soaking before it can be used. Also fairly abundant were beans - haricot beans went into a multitude of dishes as per the Ministry of Food's instruction to housewives to 'Feed them beans!'

Meat became scarcer and very expensive. Rabbit featured a lot in many guises such as in stews, pies, brawn, curried and many more. Wild ones featured, but commonly the family 'pets' were the ones to become dinner as they could be easily kept in the back yard and bred rapidly.

Tinned meat became very popular and corned beef was used imaginatively to make filling meals as was Spam, which had been launched in 1937. Tinned fish also proved very good store cupboard items, adaptable for many recipes. Pilchards and herring were particularly popular and turned up as bakes, flans, pies or devilled amongst many other ways to present them.

An advertisement for Spam in 1958 Farmhouse Fare, a book under-going many reprints but containing the same recipes, with additions, from the original 1935 edition.

Recipes tended to have less fat than modern versions of the same dish. With a rationed allowance of 2 oz (50g) butter, 4 oz (100g) margarine and 4 oz (100g) cooking fat per person per week it is easy to see that pastry or cakes would soon deplete the weekly rations. With sugar in short supply desserts also tended to be healthier - 8 oz (225g) of sugar per person, per week was the allowance. Milk and eggs were often only available in powdered form, which required reconstituting. Powdered milk was often called 'Household milk'.

An advert from the Ministry of Food showed children assisting mothers in the kitchen with the rhyme:

Household milk? Why ma that's easy;
Made this way it can't go cheesy.
First the water, then the powder.
Mothers never quite felt prouder!

Some common kitchen equipment during the War years.

This is not a long chapter, but hopefully the following recipes provide a flavour of the day!

Bubble & squeek

The modern bubble and squeek dish we know and love today was only prepared with potato along with the cabbage and other vegetable left-overs from after the First World War. Before this time it was a cabbage dish (no potato). This form of bubble and squeek was eaten from at least the early 1700s. It was a poor person's dish which could have beef added in later recipes as beef became a cheaper meat. Victorian recipes often used beef diced within the squeek and decorated around the edge with slices of roast beef.

Potato and watercress soup

½ litre (1 pint) vegetable stock*
½ litre (1 pint) reconstituted milk ('household milk' in the recipes)
450 g (1 lb) potatoes
2 bunches watercress, washed & chopped
Knob margarine
Salt & pepper to taste

Peel potatoes, cut into pieces and cook in the stock until very soft. Mash them in the pan with the back of a wooden spoon. Add milk, margarine and season to taste. Add the watercress, reheat and serve.
(*Housewives were advised to keep a soup pot on the go – adding leaves, root vegetables or anything suitable to make the stock – continuously adding vegetables or finished cooking water, ensuring it was brought to the boil once a day. This was used as a basis for a variety of soups, casseroles and sauces. I used this method here.)

Above: Potato and watercress soup. A good stock is the secret for a wonderful flavour. The soft silkiness of the soup contrasted to the crisp and peppery bite of the watercress – absolutely delicious!

Fish envelope

8 tablespoons flour
4 tablespoons mashed potato
50 g (2 oz) fat, left in warm place to soften
100 g (4 oz) cod or any tinned fish, drained
12 tablespoons cooked vegetables, a variety and mashed
½ cup fairly thick white sauce
Salt & pepper to season

Make the pastry by mixing the flour with the potato and add the fat. This will probably be fine to roll out, but add tiny amount of water if it is too dry. Divide into two pieces and roll out, placing the first piece in a suitable baking tin. Flake the fish over the bottom pastry layer, cover with the thick sauce. Drop the vegetable mix over this, or spread onto other pastry half, whichever is easier. Gently join them together into one envelope in the tin. Bake for 20 to 30 minutes at 220°C, Gas Mark 7. It can be eaten hot or cold. It is a little bland for today's palate, requiring a lot of seasoning.

Chinese cake (a bean & bacon main dish)

Haricot beans were a good source of protein when meat was scarce and as the Ministry said 'a clever cook can work wonders with them'.

675 g (1½ lb) haricot beans (if dried then soak for 24 hours) (Serves 4)
450 g (1 lb) mashed potatoes
110 g (4 oz) boiled bacon
2 teaspoons dried sage
1 teaspoon sugar
Crisp breadcrumbs (to line the tin)
Salt & pepper to taste

If using dried beans these will need cooking for 1½ hours in salted water. Mash the beans when cooked, mix with potato, the chopped bacon, sugar, sage and seasoning.

Grease a cake tin and sprinkle with the breadcrumbs to coat the sides and base. Put the mixture in the tin, firming it with the back of the spoon. Cover with greased paper and cook at 180°C for about 1 hour. Serve with selected vegetables and gravy. Surprisingly tasty.

Corned beef fritters

50 g (2 oz) flour
½ reconstituted egg (or 1 egg yolk)
15 ml (¼ pint) milk
150 g (6 oz) corned beef, finely chopped
1 teaspoon grated onion
Herbs such as teaspoon chopped parsley and/or pinch mixed herbs
Knob of dripping

Make the batter by blending the flour with milk, egg and salt. Ensure it is smooth and then add the corned beef, onion and herbs. Melt the dripping and when very hot drop in spoonfuls of the batter. Fry quickly, turning, and serve as soon as they are crisp and brown. These went down well with everyone!

Toad in the hole

Unlike other meat, sausages were not rationed – however, they were very hard to obtain.

450 g (1 lb) sausages (any type, but if scarce make lentil sausages, as below)
25 g (1 oz) dripping or lard

150 g (5 oz) plain flour
1 tablespoon dried egg powder (or 1 fresh egg if available)
300 ml (½ pint) milk – diluted with water if short of milk
Salt to season

Melt the dripping in a baking tin in an oven set to 200° C, Gas Mark 6. Add the sausages and cook for about 5 minutes, turning during this time. Increase the temperature to 200° C, Gas Mark 7 while making the batter. To make the batter mix the flour, egg and salt together and whisk in the milk (or milk/water blend). Open the oven and pour the batter mixture over the very hot sausages, closing the door again quickly and cook for 25-30 minutes. Do not open the oven door again during the cooking or the Yorkshire batter will fall flat. If it looks as though it is browning too quickly simply turn the oven down a little. Serve with a rich gravy and vegetables in season. This has survived the years and still a much-loved dish.

Lentil sausages

This recipe is the equivalent to 450 g (1 lb) sausages and should make eight.
75 g (3 oz) split lentils
1 onion
Sage and parsley, chopped; salt & pepper to season to taste
225g (8 oz) mashed potato and 1 tablespoon flour
If making Toad in the Hole then use without breadcrumbs, but to serve as sausages coat with:
Dried egg (reconstituted) or 1 fresh egg
Breadcrumbs

Cook lentils, onion, sage and seasoning with enough water to end up with a thick puree. Mix with the flour, potato and parsley. Form into sausage shapes. Use as they are for toad in the hole, or to eat in other ways coat by rolling each sausage in the beaten egg and breadcrumbs. They can be fried, grilled or baked until brown. I could not get the knack with this one and they always fell apart.

Champ

Quantities of ingredients for this wartime version of the Irish dish are to suit whatever is available and so they are approximate. Wash and slice 450 g (1 lb) of carrots and 450 g (1 lb) of potatoes. Finely shred a small cabbage. Place all three into a saucepan with about a cup of water and season generously with salt. Cook for about 15 minutes on a moderate to low heat, shaking the pan to mix occasionally. The water will have boiled away at the point the vegetables are cooked. Mash well adding a cup of hot milk and plenty of seasoning. Serve.

Marrow surprise

1 medium sized marrow, peeled and de-seeded, cut into chunks.
225 g (8 oz) carrots, sliced
Good handful of runner beans, sliced
28 g (1 oz) margarine
2 tablespoons flour
½ pint vegetable stock and reconstituted milk
100 g (4 oz) grated cheese
Salt & pepper to season

Put the carrots and the runner beans into a pan of boiling salted water. Cover and cook until almost tender before adding the prepared marrow, bring back to the boil and simmer for c. 5 minutes until cooked.
Make the cheese sauce by melting the margarine in a pan, taking it off the heat to blend in the flour. Very gradually add the stock and milk mixture, stirring continuously as it is placed back over the heat and brought back to the boil. When thick and smooth add the cheese and season to taste. Place the vegetables in a serving dish, pour over the cheese sauce and brown under the grill. Serve with potatoes. A strong cheese works best for flavour. Not sure what the surprise was meant to be!

Treacle Tart

A popular dessert, although the recipes are always with golden syrup rather than treacle! A sweet treat, very filling and a way of using up stale bread.

Shortcrust pastry
   (a 150 g (6 oz) flour mix to line a 20 cm (8 inch) flan tin)
200 g (8 oz) golden syrup
50 g (2 oz) fresh breadcrumbs
Grated rind and juice of a lemon (if you could beg, borrow or steal one!) or lemon essence

Line a tin with the pastry, keep back enough pastry for decoration. Mix the breadcrumbs, syrup and lemon and fill the pastry case. Decorate with strips of the pastry – a lattice pattern looks very attractive. Bake at 180 °C for about 20 minutes, until lightly browned. This one gave the saying 'it'll stick your ribs together' I am sure!

Chocolate layer cake with mock whipped cream

80 g (3 oz) margarine
225 g (8 oz) flour
1 teaspoon baking powder and 1 teaspoon bicarbonate of soda
1 tablespoon treacle or syrup
56 g (2 oz) sugar
½ teaspoon salt
40 g (1.5 oz) of Bourneville cocoa powder
½ pint warm water

Place the fat and syrup into a pan warming to melt the fat. Mix the dry ingredients in a mixing bowl and stir in the melted fat and syrup, adding the water until a soft consistency is formed. Place into two greased cake tins. Bake for about 30 minutes at 180ºC, Gas Mark 4. Cool and then turn the cakes out onto a plate. Sandwich together with mock cream as the filling.

Mock cream

28 g (1 oz) margarine (Serves 2 to 4 or filling for the cake above)
28 g (1 oz) sugar
1 tablespoon dried milk powder and 1 tablespoon milk.

Cream the margarine with the sugar, then beat in the milk powder and the milk. Not a very good taste, so only make this one if you are desperate for a cream substitute or inquisitive.

Dripping cake

225 g (8 oz) self raising flour with a pinch of salt
100 g (4 oz) clarified dripping (or cooking fat as available)
80 g (3 oz) sugar
1 egg (reconstituted or fresh)
150 g (5 oz) mixed dried fruit or as available
6 tablespoons of milk

Grease a 15 cm (6 inch) cake tin. Preheat oven 180oC, Gas Mark 4. Rub the dripping into the flour and then add all other ingredients. Place the mix in the cake tin and bake for about an hour to 1 hour 10 minutes. It will be firm to the touch and will turn out on to a cake rack to cool. A lovely moist cake.

17.

Horses for courses

Looking through the glimpse provided by this book on our changing diet, our cookery methods, menus and recipes it seems as though we have come full circle. Palaeolithic diets were simple with lots of greens, nuts, berries, fruit, insects, meat if you could find it – in fact anything you could find and safely eat. Subsequent farming in the Neolithic led to a massive change in the amount of time we saved on hunting and gathering to find sufficient food to survive – thus leaving time for the ceremonial and artistic side of life. From here we progressed through a series of agricultural crop improvements – genetic engineering started early on by simply selecting those crops and animals with the best traits for our purposes. This could include things as variable as better beef animals to heavier cropping fruit trees or fatter grain that does not require as much processing.

As we started trading with other cultures, this automatically resulted in an expansion of the range of items in our diet. Technology developed in a similar way with influences from other cultures. As a result we produced new tools and new ways of cooking. Innovations occurred in every period – we are a species that enjoys inventing and it is even better if those inventions make life easier. However, as food became easier to get hold of (for some anyway) this led us to make bad choices. Our downfall has always been our natural desire for sweet and rich foods. As a hunter gatherer the rare finds of these items ensured survival – that is why we have the 'taste and desire' gene steering us to choose sweet and fatty foods. However, a constant and abundant supply of these calorific foods simply ensures overweight individuals and rotten teeth, amidst a range of other health problems. By the Tudor period we were well and truly down that sorrowful path.

Several eras started health movements. The Romans started ideas of health based on the 'humours' which continued through to Victorian times. The Stuart eagerness for simplicity was based on ethical desires for austerity being the correct way to live. However, after this period the fashion turned to desiring more meat, more sugar and much more refined food, thus removing the goodness afforded by fibre. This was partly taste driven but also the wish to show off wealth through food and the elaborate presentation of that food. The Victorians finally observed the connection between diet and health. By the end of the Victorian period healthy changes began to come into play such as wholemeal bread coming back into the diet – sometimes in an almost 'medicinal' way. The Victorians also saw the influence of colonialism with increasing foods and recipes influenced by the countries we ruled. India for instance provided spice combinations and dishes which have continued to grow to almost a passion. Indian food is arguably our most favourite food today.

However, throughout our human history it is seen that at times of war our diet is no longer at the whim of preferences, taste, price or fashion. When food supplies are interrupted by war, diet becomes whatever you can get hold of. The Second World War showed great ingenuity at making wholesome food from very little, but intriguing in the way that 'mock' dishes were so popular. People were almost trying to retain the memory of foods that were special to them in pre-war times. Confirming that food is, without doubt, also good for mental health – providing the feeling of well-being even when you are still hungry!

So where do we go from here? Today, more than ever, we have easy, abundant food sources. These sources are relatively cheaper than they have ever been thanks to modern technology and high yield crops resulting from thousands of years of genetic selection for the best varieties. However, it seems that not all is rosy in the modern Homo sapiens' diet. One problem is a hugely increasing population worldwide. Future food supplies may well be in jeopardy for other reasons too. Global warming will disrupt what we are able to grow, where we are able to grow it, and the quantities that can be grown successfully as we encounter more extremes in seasonal weather.

Methods of intensive farming have led to many older varieties of animal and plant being lost. There are many institutions around the world taking on the role of maintaining seed banks of heritage varieties of fruit, vegetables and grain and also a strong commitment to maintain ancient breeds of animal. Heritage varieties have disappeared exceptionally quickly which is a great shame for many reasons including taste, providing a range of choice, resistance to diseases and maintaining a gene bank with genetic variety.

Heritage apple Reinette do Canada Grise grown at Le Manoir Aux Quat' Saison. This is an 18th century dessert apple. Fruit as well as a multitude of vegetables is now taking on a more scientific approach to propagating both heritage and new delicious varieties. Agricultural catalogues grew in popularity during the Victorian period and, as an example, the variety of apples alone had risen to more than a thousand during that time. Valuable heritage seed work is carried out by Kew and by Ryton Organic Gardens.

Today we are much more tuned in to knowledge of healthy eating – but a good proportion of the population is still addicted to the sweet and the rich food choices. However, there seems a sense of another food movement afoot – growing more locally, eating more seasonably, with less meat, less sugar, more pulses, and many more greens. This is all beginning to sound like our hunter-gatherer starting point. Are we about to come full circle? Maybe! Meat eaters are already eating more body parts of the animals slaughtered – not just the prime cuts. So offal has made a very fashionable come-back. Not just kidneys, liver or heart – all included in many eras. Recently on menus were pig's ears, trotters and chicken gizzards – all eaten and enjoyed recently in restaurants and they were absolutely delicious.

However, there are some taboos that remain entrenched in societies – for instance pork for Muslims or beef for Hindus. In Britain horsemeat is generally not on the menus of choice. According to research by Dr Poole of Nottingham University this could be that horses were associated with various pagan gods in northwest Europe, leading to them being eaten for religious reasons only. However, we were happy to eat horsemeat in 7th century pagan Anglo-Saxon England. When Christianity was introduced in the 8th century it was suddenly dropped as food, and has been a distasteful idea to the English ever since.

Changes in food supply are already leading to investigations of farming krill as a food source, and insects may be purchased as food on-line today. Both these sources of highly nutritious food are heralded as potential saviours capable of supplying quality protein, minerals and calories to growing populations. This all begins to show our dietary fashions and fancies coming back full circle to a more nutritious form of our Palaeolithic diet. The difference being that this time round it is more regularly available. Maybe recent changes will see more horses for courses! We can only watch and see. Whichever direction our diet takes next, there is one thing that I am sure will never change – cheers!

"Ask not what you can do for your country. Ask what's for lunch."   **Orson Welles**

Further reading

Beeton, Isabella. 1861. *Mrs Beeton's book of household management.* Reprinted by Skyhorse Publishing.

Beeton, Isabella 1909. *Mrs Beeton's all about cookery.* Ward, Lock & Co. London.

Black. M. 2004. *Victorian cookery: Recipes and History.* English Heritage.

Cool, H. E. M. 2006. *Eating and drinking in Roman Britain.* Cambridge University Press.
An excellent book with lots of detail and many references to find out more.

Mabey, R. 2012. *Food for free.* Harper Colins, London. ISBN 978-0-00-743847-1.
An excellent guide to identifying edible species of the UK, with recipes.

Patten, Marguerite 2002. *Victory cookbook.* Octopus Publishing Group with Imperial War Museum.

Ray Mears and Gordon Hillman. 2008. *Wild food.* Hodder. ISBN 978-0-340-82791-8
Based on a BBC television programme and particularly good for the Mesolithic diet.

Roberts, Jonathon 2001. *Cabbages and Kings: the origins of fruit and vegetables.* Harper Collins, London ISBN 0 002202077

Spencer, Colin. 2011. *British Food: an extraordinary thousand years of history.* Grub Street, London.

Taylor, Randal 1664. *The Court and kitchen of Elizabeth commonly called Joan Cromwell, The wife of the late Usurper, Truly described and represented, and now made public for general satisfaction.* St Martins Le Grand.

Vindolanda on-line. An excellent source of the writing tablets with images and translations.
www.vindolanda.csad.ox.ac.uk

Woolgar, C. H., Serjeantson, D. and Waldron, T. 2006. *Food in Medieval England: Diet and nutrition.* Oxford University Press.

Bibliography

Colledge, S. and Conolly,J. 2014. Wild plant use in European Neolithic subsistence economies: a formal assessment of preservation bias in archaeobotanical assemblages and the implications for understanding changes in plant diet breadth. *Quaternary Science Reviews* **101:** 193-206.

Eyers, J. *St Dunstan's Church, Monks Risborough, Bucks: Archaeological excavation – graveyard extension.* Chiltern Archaeology Report No. 130.

Green, M. J. 1998. Vessels of death: sacred cauldrons in archaeology and myth. *Antiquaries Journal,* **78:** 63-84.

Hardy *et al.* 2016. Diet and environment 1.2 million years ago revealed through analysis of dental calculus from Europe's oldest hominin at Sima del Elefante, Spain. *Science of Nature Journal* accessed on-line 23.12.2016; doi:10.1007/s00114-016-1420-x.

Hedges, R, Saville, A and O'Connell, T. 2008. Characterizing the diet of individuals at the Neolithic chambered tomb of Hazleton North, Gloucestershire, England, using stable isotopic analysis *Archaeometry* **50, 1:** 114–128.

John A.J. Gowlett & Richard W. Wrangham. 2013. Earliest fire in Africa: towards the convergence of archaeological evidence and the cooking hypothesis, *Azania: Archaeological Research in Africa*, **48:1**, 5-30, DOI: 10.1080/0067270X.2012.756754

Mahoney, P. 2007. Human dental microwear from Ohalo II (22,500–23,500 cal BP), southern Levant. *American Journal of Physical Anthropology*, **132(4)**, 489-500.

Milner, N, Craig, O. E, Bailey, G. N, Pedersen, K. & Andersen, S. H. 2004. Something fishy in the Neolithic? A re-evaluation of stable isotope analysis of Mesolithic and Neolithic coastal populations. *Antiquity* **78**: 9-22.

Power, Robert C ; Salazar-García, Domingo C ; Straus, Lawrence G; González Morales, Manuel R; Henry, Amanda G. 2015. Microremains from El Mirón Cave human dental calculus suggest a mixed plant–animal subsistence economy during the Magdalenian in Northern Iberia. *J. Archaeological Science*, **60**, 39-46.

Revedin et al. 2010. Thirty thousand-year-old evidence of plant food processing. *Proc Natl Acad Sci U S A.* **107(44)**: 18815–18819.

Richards, M.P; Hedges, R.E.M; Jacobi, R; Current, A; Stringer, C. 2000. Gough's Cave and Sun Hole Cave Human Stable Isotope Values Indicate a High Animal Protein Diet in the British Upper Palaeolithic. *Journal of Archaeological Science*, **27(1)**, 1-3.

Richards, M.P; Jacobi, R ; Cook, J ; Pettitt, P.B ; Stringer, C.B. 2005. Isotope evidence for the intensive use of marine foods by Late Upper Palaeolithic humans. *Journal of Human Evolution*, **49(3)**, pp.390-394.

Turner, R. 1999. *Excavations of an Iron Age and Roman religious complex at Ivy Chimneys, Witham, Essex 1978-1983*. EAA **88**: Chelmsford.

Classical writers used in the book

Anthimus: Greek doctor and author of *De observatione ciborum* (On the Observance of Foods), writing c. 490-500 AD.

Atheneaus: died 192 AD. A Greek and author of at least 15 volumes almost entirely dedicated to the art of dining. The topics not only include food, but music, dancing, banqueting, courtesans and games – everything required for the first-class dining experience.

Cato: 234-149 BC. A Roman statesman whose literary works include *De Agri Cultura* (a farming manual with bread recipes) and *De Re Rustica* discusses the cultivation of produce such as vines, fruit and olives, written from his own experience.

Cicero: 106-43 BC a writer of a vast amount of literature and whose letters are very revealing of life and customs in the Roman Empire.

Dio Cassius (*also known as Cassius Dio*): 150-235 AD. His accounts of the Roman Empire including 80 books on the history of Rome are informative about many aspects of life and death at this time.

Galen (Galenus): a Greek physician working in modern day Turkey, c. 129-200/216 AD.

Hippocrates: 460-370 BC. A Greek physician notable for his texts on medicine and health.

Pliny the Elder: 23-79 AD. His 37 books on natural history and other topics are well known today.

Pliny the Younger: 61-113 AD. Wrote a large number of letters covering life during this period.

Tacitus: 56-117 AD. A Gaul who became a Roman Senator. His numerous works describe events, tribes and customs that have influenced other writers since.

Varro: 116-27 BC. Much information in his 600 books on a wide variety of topics, but his De Rustica (3 books) describes farming (written for his wife Fundania).

"How can you govern a country which has 246 varieties of cheese?" **Charles de Gaulle**

Some important food dates

Years ago:

1 million?	Human groups learn how to make fire and cooking was an early use of this resource.
30,000	30,000 years ago crushed grain is made into a paste and baked – the first flatbread.
10,000	By 10,000 years ago grain and bread became a staple food.
2,800	Plum stones found in Iron Age levels of Maiden Castle – introduction or trading?
2, 043	Romans brought cucumbers, leeks, and a huge variety of other fruit & vegetables & herbs.

Date:

1100	Pasta finds its way into British food with the Normans (initially provided from the Arabs).
1200s	Sugar began to be imported and began replacing honey for sweetening for the rich.
1275	Redcurrants, blackcurrants and gooseberries being grown (from wild German source).
1390	The first cookery book, as we know it, written for Richard II *The Forme of Cury*.
1525	Turkeys introduced to UK from the Americas. Cod became the favourite fish.
1550s	Kidney beans introduced to Britain from the New World.
1568	First known raspberry in UK, but wild relatives may have existed in Scotland earlier.
1540	Tomatoes had been brought to Europe by the Spanish, soon to reach English tables.
1580s	Melons introduced to England by the late 1500s.
1580s	Potatoes arrived in Britain, along with tea from China, pepper from India, cinnamon from Ceylon, nutmeg, mace, cloves & other spices from many islands, red beetroot from Italy.
1580s	The British get hold of the cocoa bean from the Spanish – we can now drink hot chocolate!
1600	About this date the orange carrot appears – wild carrots were white or purple up till this time.
Mid-1600s	Chocolate was introduced to England from Mexico. Rhubarb imported from Asia.
1737	The first recipe for Yorkshire pud called 'Dripping pudding' in *The whole duty of a woman*.
1762	The sandwich is invented by the Fourth Earl of Sandwich.
Late 1700s	The French started outdoor eating (the pique-nique) with friends each bringing something along to share. Anything French was instantly fashionable – hence our picnic was born.
1822	William Kitchener attributed as 'inventing' the chip.
1834	Bottled lemonade is produced by Schweppes.
1845	The Duchess of Bedford 'invented' afternoon tea.
1847	Fry's produce their first chocolate.
1876	Tomato ketchup is first produced by Heinz; Camp coffee first produced.
1880	Baked beans were produced in the UK; desiccated coconut first produced.

1880s	Golden syrup was first made as a by-product of refining crystallised sugar.
1881	Loganberries produced by J. H. Logan
1885	The Nantes carrot was grown for the first time
1893	Shredded wheat invented by Henry D Perky, perfected later by Kelloggs, paying no royalty.
1896	HP sauce brand name was registered (HP = Houses of Parliament, where it was avidly eaten!)
1902	Marmite comes into production.
1905	Cadbury's produce their first bar of Dairy Milk chocolate.
1912	Rohwedder invented a machine to slice bread, used in1928 when bread could also be wrapped
1922	The first packet of crisps is produced by Smith's.
1934	Coca Cola brought their bottled coke to the UK.
1937	Spam introduced to the market place along with Bird's custard powder.
1960s	The term Ploughman's Lunch was invented for a meal of bread, cheese & pickles, often eaten in a pub!
1962	Heinz tomato soup launched in Britain.
1967	Angel Delight launched onto the dessert scene.

Places to visit

Belmond Le Manoir aux Quat'Saisons, Church Road, Great Milton, Oxford, OX44 7PD.
An excellent hotel and restaurant in a beautiful setting, growing heritage varieties of fruit and vegetables.

The lavender avenue at Le Manoir

Butser Ancient Farm, Chalton Lane, Chalton, Waterlooville, Hampshire, PO8 0BG.
An experimental archaeology site with buildings showing stone age, Iron Age, Roman and Anglo-Saxon construction and life-style, with wonderful displays and activity days.

A reconstructed Iron Age hut at Butser

Oliver Cromwell's House, 29 St Mary's Street,, Ely, Cambridgeshire,, CB7 4H.
Oliver Cromwell's former home showing the life-style of the day.

National Trust, nationaltrust.org.uk
For a multitude of historic houses (with their kitchens and kitchen gardens), farms and other buildings across the country.

Ryton Organic Gardens
Wolston Lane, Ryton on Dunsmore, Coventry, CV8 3LG. *www.rytongardens.org.uk*
Gardens, courses, café, heritage vegetable garden, herb garden and biodynamics.

Sally Lunn's, Bath
4 North Parade Passage, Bath, BA1 1NX. *www.sallylunns.co.uk*
An authentic English eating house and kitchen museum famous for selling the little Sally Lunn buns.

Pitstone Green Museum of Rural Life
Pitstone, Bucks, LU7 9EY. Displays of aspects of rural life from village areas surrounding the museum.
www.pitstonemuseum.co.uk

St Katharine's Parmoor, Frieth, Buckinghamshire
A superb setting for retreats, accommodation, seminars, talks and conferences in a tranquil and beautiful setting.
http://www.srpf.org.uk/about.html

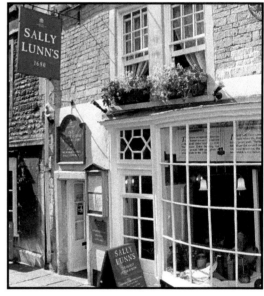

Verulamium Museum, St Albans, Herts
An excellent Roman Museum and the excavated site of Roman Verulamium.

Sally Lunn's Historic Eating House, Bath

West Stow Anglo-Saxon Village, Icklingham Road, West Stow, Suffolk, IP28 6HG.
A reconstructed Saxon village showing the lifestyle and with events and activity days.

Yorvik Viking centre, Coppergate, York
A reconstruction of the streets of Viking York on the site of on-going excavations.

House at West Stowe

Roman food items

Asafoetida root has a very strong flavour and only tiny amounts are needed. The English name is 'The Devil's Dung'! Indian shops and some chemists stock it.

Defructum: a concentrated grape juice which is very sweet. Wine-making suppliers often stock it and some large chemists such as Boots. If stuck use ordinary grape juice instead. It was used to sweeten dishes instead of honey.

Liquamen, Garum, Muriae and Allec: varieties of fish sauce (liquamen is the clearest; Allec is sediment). A substitute can be a strong Thai fish sauce or Burgess' Anchovy sauce, both acceptable in the Roman recipes.

Anglo-Saxon and Norman words in recipes

Alay	To mix
Anys	Aniseed/fennel?
Brede	Bread
Canel	Cinnamon
Clowes	Cloves
Cofyns	Pastry cases
Cursey	A cup
Galyngale	a spice from ground Cypress tree root (from Asian shops or substitute with pepper)
Hem	Them or it
Hew/hewe	To chop
Mary bones	Marrow bones
Messe	To serve (the term is usually 'messe it forth')
Þe	The
Perboyle	Also spelt Parboyle is to parboil (partly cook it by boiling)
Postnet	Pot
Pottle	A quantity = 2 litres or 4 pints
Rys	Rice
Schiveris	Aspic?
Seeth/seth	To boil
Serpell	Wild thyme
Sle	Sloe?
Streyn	Strain
Ynow	Enough

Acknowledgements

I am very grateful to all the following: my lovely friend Judy Barber who allowed access to her personal library of useful books, allowing me to rummage through her cupboards and take away lots of props from many eras for photographing cooked food dishes; the staff at Ryton Organic Gardens for showing me the grounds and the wonderful work they undertake on heritage seeds; Anne Marie Owens at Le Manoir de Quatres Saisons who provided access to the gardens and to their heritage varieties of fruit, vegetables and herbs; Lacey's Farm shop, Bolter End Farm, Lane End, HP14 3LP for providing top quality meat and Guernsey milk which made the recipes much more authentic when testing; Brett Thorn keeper of the archaeological collections at the Buckinghamshire County Museum for finding lovely treasures to photograph. Last, but not least, thanks to Dave Biggs of CPI Anthony Rowe for his excellent advice and assistance.

For more information, courses or to book a talk contact:
Chiltern Archaeology: day courses for the public, as well as books and leaflets of interest on a variety of archaeological topics. *www.chilternarchaeology.com*

The recipe testers at work Roman style